BEE'S ADVENTURES IN CAKE DECORATING

BEE'S ADVENTURES IN CAKE DECORATING

HOW TO MAKE CAKES WITH THE WOW FACTOR

BEE BERRIE

PAVILION

This book is for my main man Dan, the Yorkshireman.
Thank you for the amazing road trips, being my wonderful
wingman and your expert-level planning capabilities.
I can't wait for our next little adventure . . .

CONTENTS

INTRODUCTION

In 2016, my first ever recipe book, *Bee's Brilliant Biscuits*, launched in the UK, Australia, Canada and the USA, and – wow – what a wild ride it was! Creating the "holy grail of biscuit baking" was such an incredibly cool experience that I thought I'd have another crack at it! So, here goes . . .

This time, we're talking cakes and cake decorating; so, welcome, my caped cake crusaders, my decorating demons, to the baddest cake-baking book in town!

Let's 'fess up to the truth: most home bakers know about the power of the classic sponge cake, and can knock out a pretty worthy creation without too much effort. So, how do you make your designs stand out from the rest of the Bake Off generation's creations? By thinking outside of the cake box, that's how.

I'm not an artistic person – that's a fact. I studied microbiology at university and worked in medical science for years before even lifting up a palette knife. Because of this, the right side of my brain feels woefully underdeveloped, and I really struggled to find the confidence to get creative with my designs when I first set up the bakery, in 2012. I soon learned, though, that capturing a little flicker of an idea from another source, and letting it grow and build into an idea of my own, is what works for me. Looking at art (I'm talking print design, typography and illustrators on Instagram, here – not the old masters!), listening to the words in songs, forcing myself to learn the colours of the rainbow – these all spark ideas, which turn into cakes and bakes with personality.

For a stack of inspirational ideas and some tips on getting creative, check out page 12.

This book covers many of the basic skills needed to make a great cake, from my favourite core sponge recipes and frostings, to tips and techniques on how to get straight edges when icing. There are instructions for making cool cake stands and funky cake toppers from scratch, and some fiddlier techniques to make your own paper and sugar flowers. Learn about the power of the piping bag and how to bring an old-fashioned technique, like making buttercream flowers, right up to date.

⊳⊳

There are recipes for cakes made from store-cupboard essentials, wonky veg and vegan cakes, tons of different icing and frosting recipes, and there's even a cake made with beer! The ideas can be adapted for birthdays, weddings, baby showers and parties, for summertime and winter and everything in between. I'll also show you what to do with leftover/broken cake pieces.

My business has grown out of a genuine happiness at being in the kitchen. Whilst building a business itself isn't always fun, creating, baking and selling cakes and cookies most definitely is. At my old job, I daydreamed about baking beautiful wedding cakes for couples at venues all over London, and I'm thrilled that now I get to bake for amazing clients such as Selfridges and Harrods, plus venues such as Kew Gardens, the Rosewood Hotel, Wilton's Music Hall, Burgh House and Ham Yard Hotel.

I really believe in the calming power of smashing a delicious recipe out in the kitchen. Working up a sweat works wonders in clearing my tiny mind of the admin junk that accumulates whilst running my own business, and I expect it could calm your mind too. The kitchen is definitely my "happy place", and I hope that the recipes and ideas in this book help you tap into your own version of what I call "bake love".

So, get up, get your bake face on and have a go! I'd love you to get in touch, and ask any questions you have, on social media. My handle is @beesbakery on Twitter and Instagram, and I'd love to see pics of your creations, so tag me using #BeesAdventuresInCake.

Bee x

SUPER HOT TIPS FOR EXTRA COOL BAKING

1. Turn into a planning beast and get organized in advance – especially for bigger baking projects or more complicated cakes.

2. Get some baking biceps! Engage your abs and arm muscles, and only cheat with a mixer if you really need to – after all, you might have a couple of extra calories to burn off afterwards!

3. Try to use the best quality ingredients that you can afford; it really will make your cakes taste better. Always use free-range eggs – healthier and happier hens lay better eggs.

4. Don't overwork yourself, or the cake mixture. Too much mixing and beating can knock air bubbles out of your cake, resulting in flat or wonky cake layers.

5. Get the tunes on! A baking playlist will keep you going when the bake gets tough.

6. Don't be afraid to tidy up any gammy bits of your cakes when they come out of the oven – carefully chop off any burnt bits, straighten a wonky edge with a serrated knife, or hide any knobbly bits with icing – and make your cakes look beautiful!

7. Get thrifty with your offcuts / extra cake batter. If you have leftover batter, bake a little 4- or 6-inch cake layer, then freeze it for use later – maybe combining with other cake layers you might have (see pages 126–129 for ideas of what to do with leftover cake trimmings).

8. Get friendly with your oven – understand its hot spots so you know which shelf bakes the best cakes.

9. Improvise with your kit. Save the boxes your cling-film comes in and use them to block off the edges of your big rectangular cake tins to get smaller squares. So what if you don't have the snazziest cake scraper? Make your own out of the bottom of a margarine tub. If you can't stretch to an expensive, fancy-pants cake stand, just make your own (using our guide on page 134). Who cares if you don't have a collection of posh fabric piping bags? Make your own by snipping a little hole from the corner of a ziplock bag filled with icing, or by making a cone from a triangle of parchment paper.

10. Be creative by taking your favourite classic recipe and making your own adjustments – try new flavour combinations or play with colours.

11. Gift single slices of cake, boxed up all pretty and tied with ribbon. This'll make you super popular and prevent you from getting a baker's belly!

12. Keep frozen and wrapped slices of cake in the freezer and rustle up a delicious slice of cake by just defrosting at room temperetaure for about 20 minutes.

WHERE TO LOOK FOR CREATIVE INSPIRATION

I find it pretty hard to switch on my creativity button sometimes, and often look for a spark of inspiration from another source before I turn it into a brilliant cake idea. Here's a list of places I go when I need to find a flicker of an idea for a colour, shape, texture or style.

Print design. I particularly love wrapping paper from Paperchase, House of Hackney, Liberty and William Morris.

Pinterest/Instagram. Have a look for ideas from other countries and cultures. For example, cake designers from Japan and Malaysia are really incredible.

Patterns on gift wrap/greetings cards' design. My failsafe is the Liberty stationery shop, which has many of its designs online, but I also go to illustration and print design trade fairs too.

Nature and seasonal colours. Get out in the green!

Florists. I am deeply in love with the styles and skills of some florists that I know, and their abilities to put together the most striking bouquets I've ever seen. Check out @Wild_Renata_Flowers, @WormLondon and @AugustusBloom on Instagram.

Pantone and paint charts. True story!

The actual colours of the rainbow and colour wheels. Essential for a scientist trying to understand which colours go together.

Illustrators and modern art. I follow a bunch of illustrators on Instagram, including @CamilleWalala, @JollyAwesomeArt and @Jimbobart.

Colouring pencils and pens. Having a full-colour set of either pens or pencils really helps me to imagine how colour combinations on cakes will look in reality.

Favourite shapes. Mine are triangles and hexagons.

Clothes shops and brands with wacky patterns. I find it inspiring to look at the window displays of stores I love, e.g. Carhartt or Lazy Oaf, to get ideas on shapes, patterns and textures that I can carry over into decorating my cakes.

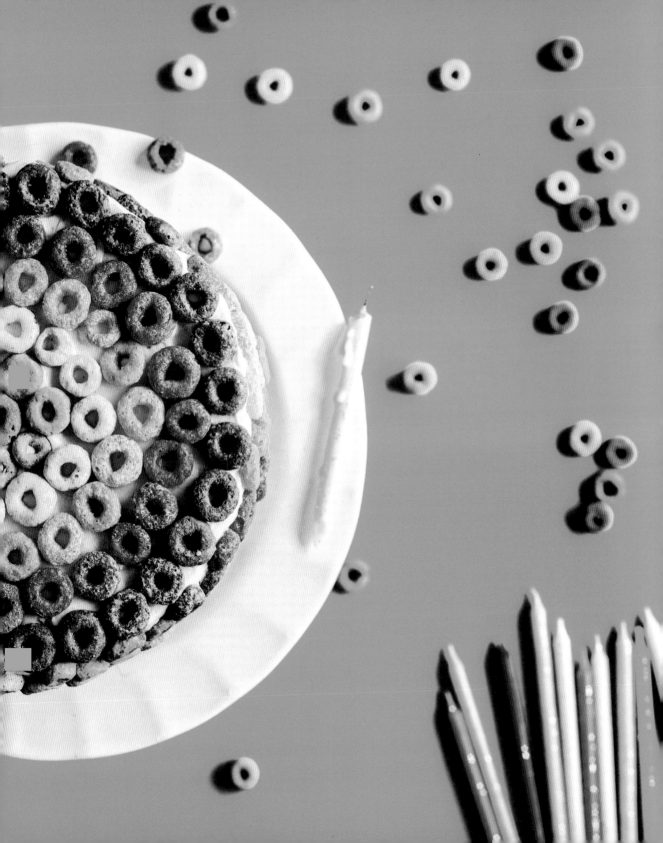

Q & A / TROUBLESHOOTING

These are the things I get asked most frequently. If you have other questions, look me up on Twitter and Instagram @beesbakery and ask away!

Q: What's better for lining cake tins, butter and flour, or parchment?
A: I use parchment, as it's less messy and it also provides a protective layer between the cake and the tin, which means that the sponge colours a wee bit less when baking.

Q: How do I bake a cake with a nice flat top, so I don't need to trim it and waste cake?
A: Aha – this is a good one! First up, make sure that the batter is spread all the way to the edges of the tin, and make a little well in the centre. Then cut a circle of parchment and place it on top before baking – it sticks fast, meaning that the cake, when it rises, can't go crazy and create a dome shape. However, don't forget that, even if you do need to trim your cakes, there are two recipes for leftover cake crumbs on pages 126 and 128.

Q: Why do my cakes burn at the bottom, but stay raw in the middle?
A: Thanks for this question, Mum! First up, double-line your baking tin with good-quality parchment paper to create a barrier. If your cake is burnt on the outside/bottom/top, then, in general, the temperature is too high, or the heat is coming directly from the grill or bottom of the oven. Check that you know which setting is which – you want a fan setting for baking cakes, ideally. Bake at the minimum temperature on the recipe and, if you know your oven bakes at a hotter temperature than it says on the dial, turn it down by 5–10 degrees.

Then, get friendly with your oven! Next time you bake/cook something, have a careful look at what comes out of the oven – you might find that certain areas of your oven run hotter than others, e.g. where the fan blows the hot air out. Bear this in mind when baking cakes; move the shelf down a little, place your cake slightly to the left or right and, if the fan blows out of one side, turn your cake around part-way through baking so the top doesn't come out wonky.

Q: What difference does it make which oven shelf I use?
A: It makes tons of difference! Hot air rises, so the top of your oven will always be hotter than the bottom. Learn where your oven's hot and cool spots are and you should quickly be able to find the perfect position for an evenly baked cake.

Q: My cake always sinks in the middle – why?
A: Hmmm . . . This could be for a couple of reasons. Make sure that you don't open the oven door to check on the cake until at least 15 minutes into the baking time – a quick change in temperature or a bang of the door can shock the cake and cause it to sink. Are you letting the mixture sit for too long after mixing, but before baking it? If so, then the raising agent will have more time to get working, meaning that you might get a big air bubble in the middle. Make sure you put the mixture straight into the oven as soon as it's ready to avoid this. If you're using raising agent in the recipe, it might be that you're using too much, so try adding a little less baking powder and give it another whirl.

Q: When baking a layer cake, should I bake one big, tall cake and slice it into layers, or several smaller layers?
A: The latter – several smaller layers will bake more quickly and be more moist and tasty. Baking one big, tall cake takes ages, and the cake will be much drier.

Q: How do I make sure that my layers bake to even heights, so I don't have to trim them?
A: This is a great question, and it brings up a problem that's extra easy to fix. Measure the total weight of your ready-to-bake cake batter and divide it up by the number of layers you want. It's a bit fiddly, but is guaranteed to work and, if you're baking a naked cake, your layer heights will be nice and even.

Q: How do you keep cakes moist?
A: First up, choose a moist recipe – one with lots of liquid, e.g. beer cake, or chocolate orange milkshake cake. Secondly, either bake the cake the same day you need it, or the night before. Once it is baked and cooled, double wrap tightly with cling film, making sure there are no gaps where air can get in. If you need to bake the cake more than a day in advance, consider freezing it. Do not store it in the fridge, as the airflow can zap a cake of moisture.

Q: Do you do anything different when baking wedding cakes?
A: Yes, absolutely! For a start, I bake giant slabs of cake, rather than cakes the exact size I need them, which means that I trim off the edges and sides of each cake layer before layering them up. A really important party deserves only the very best cake, and no crispy edges, sides or tops at all – just the fluffiest, tastiest sponge possible. I also use the finest ingredients I can source, e.g. organic eggs, flour, butter and the best quality chocolate and jam that I can find. Without a doubt, it adds to the taste and quality of the cake.

Q: How can I stop my fruit sinking when I bake a fruitcake?
A: This answer applies to anything chunky that's added into a cake, really – e.g. big chunks of chocolate, or soft fruits like blueberries, etc. Basically, you need to make sure that all chopped pieces are roughly the same size – otherwise the bigger, fatter, heavier ones will sink like stones to the bottom.

Q: How can I stop my tiered cakes being wonky?
A: Some people swear by using a spirit level when they layer up their cakes, but I tend to just get down on a level with my cake, at the layering stage, to make sure that each layer looks straight, before I stack it up. Also, using strong supporting dowels or jumbo straws is really important with tiers, as it spreads the weight and avoids any leaning cakes (see image on page 77).

Q: What can you do with cake trimmings / broken cakes?
A: Lots of things – never throw them away; it's a terrible waste! I'd suggest that you put them into a ziplock bag and store them in the freezer until you have a few handfuls. Then check out my recipes for using up cake crumbs (pages 126 and 128).

Q: What's the best way to store cake?
A: In my opinion, in an airtight container, like a cake tin or Tupperware. You can also store baked cakes in the freezer for up to a month – in fact, I keep pre-cut slices of cake in the freezer, as they take only about 20 minutes to defrost . . . Argh! Now I've revealed my guilty secret. Busted!

Q: How long can you store a baked cake without icing it?
A: If the cake is wrapped in cling film, then technically (according to the microbiology lab) around 2–3 days, depending on the recipe you use (some are drier than others). However, I don't like leaving cakes for this long before serving them, so I sometimes freeze them in advance. It's something I've just started doing and, I have to say, I do think it improves the flavour and consistency, and keeps the cake super moist. You can freeze for around 1 month, maximum.

Q: What is a "crumb coat"?
A: A crumb coat is a first, light coating of icing, which is then chilled before another, thicker layer is added. It's not essential, but icing with a crumb coat first helps to seal in all of the pesky crumbs, so they can't be seen once the cake is fully decorated. You can also use it to cover any blemishes, such as little holes in the cake, so that you have a lovely, even, smooth base layer upon which to ice the final coat.

Q: When I decorate a semi-naked or naked cake, how can I stop the crumbs from the cake speckling the surface of the buttercream?
A: Aha – this is really annoying. I feel your pain! First of all, set aside a little bit of buttercream that you'll only use for the first crumb-coat layer. Cover half of your cake first, then scrape off, then reuse this crumbed-up buttercream on the other half of the cake. Then use fresh buttercream for your final layer, on top of the sealed crumb coat. This works for both semi-naked and naked cakes.

Q: What's the best icing to use on a hot day?
A: It's easier to say which icing not to use! I always avoid cream-cheese frosting on a hot day; it's too soft to rely on. Avoid Swiss meringue buttercream and stick to regular real-butter icing. Store cakes in the fridge, transport them in an ice box or with ice packs, and display for no more than 2 hours before cutting.

Q: What gluten-free cake flour do you use? How do you substitute gluten-free for regular flour in a recipe?
A: This is a super-simple one – basically, make your own mixture with a maximum of one-third pre-mixed gluten-free flour. My own is a mixture of the following: self-raising pre-mixed flour, ground chickpea flour (just a little; it has a strong flavour), ground almonds, rice flour or buckwheat flour. You might want to consider using gluten-free baking powder and gluten-free xanthan gum too, to add extra rise and ensure a well-bound texture. One more tip: I tend to recommend gluten-free recipes that carry intense flavours, to mask the often chemical taste of pre-mixed gluten-free flour. Chocolate cakes are ideal, and adding a drop of two of orange, almond or lemon essence often works well too.

Q: How do you turn plain flour into self-raising?
A: Technically, the way to do this is to add 2 level teaspoons of baking powder to every 150 g of plain flour. I'd also suggest sifting your plain flour well, with the baking powder, or whisking it to ensure that it's really evenly distributed.

Q: How do I make a vegan cake?
A: The simplest answer is . . . by following our recipe for the vegan layered cake on page 90 and the vegan banana cake on page 50. I also have some awesome vegan frosting recipes on page 40.

Q: What's the best, super-quick recipe to make with kids?
A: I have the perfect, one-bowl wonder of a recipe that's ideal for baking with kids on page 20. Try to encourage them to add in a couple of small handfuls of an ingredient they've never tried before – e.g. dried fruit/nuts/citrus zest – to keep things interesting and experiment with new flavours.

BEE'S FAVOURITE CAKE RECIPES

ONE-BOWL WONDER VANILLA SPONGE

MAKES TWO LAYERS OF 20-CM/8-INCH ROUND CAKE

220 g/7¾ oz/1 cup very soft
   butter (blast in the microwave
   for a few seconds if needed)
   or soft vegetable margarine
4 eggs
220 g/7¾ oz/1⅛ cups caster
   (superfine) sugar
220 g/7¾ oz/1¾ cups self-raising
   flour, sifted (if you have the
   time, not essential)
1 tsp good-quality vanilla-bean
   extract

This cake is a true one-bowl, one-spoon wonder that even someone with zero baking skills can take on and win at, every time! The recipe is easy to adapt too, so you can make your own mark on it. It's a brilliant recipe to make with kids.

Do use super-soft butter, or margarine – this is crucial, so ignore my warnings at your own peril! Margarine works really well in this cake, and is useful if you need to bake something that's dairy free.

Preheat your oven to 160°C/350°F/gas 4 and line two 20-cm/8-inch round baking tins with good-quality parchment. Throw all of your ingredients into a large bowl, then, using a bit of bicep strength, combine everything together in one go. Scrape the sides of the bowl down and make sure that it is mixed until there are no lumpy bits. If you want to use a mixer, mix thoroughly on a medium speed until combined, scraping down the sides as you mix.

Pour your mixture into the two tins, spreading it evenly, all the way to the edges, and make a slight well in the middle to ensure the cakes bake to an even height. Bake for around 20–25 minutes, until the sponge bounces back when pressed and a cocktail stick inserted into the cake comes out clean.

Serve with your favourite jam and a pile of buttercream, or use it as the base for any of the decoration projects in the book.

Adaptations and creative ideas
Try adding:

- A herb and citrus combination at the beginning of mixing, e.g. 2 tbsp chopped basil/rosemary/thyme/mint, alongside 2 tbsp orange, lemon or tangerine zest.
- 1-2 tbsp finely chopped flowers or herbs, such as culinary grade lavender, or rose petals, or a large splash of rosewater or orange flower water.
- A teaspoon of ground spice to add depth, e.g. cinnamon, cardamom, ground ginger, or even a pinch of chilli powder.
- A double shot of prosecco and a handful of crushed fresh fruit, e.g. raspberries, to the batter.
- Two shots of espresso coffee, substituting the caster sugar for muscovado sugar, will give a browner cake with a little more depth of flavour.
- A swirl of nut butter, e.g. almond or peanut, to the batter, and a large handful of grated chocolate sprinkled on top.
- The contents of an Earl Grey teabag (we use Joe's Tea) soaked for 5 mins in a ¼ cup of hot milk before adding.
- 2 tbsp of seeds, e.g. chia, poppyseeds or millet, to give a cool speckled effect to the sponge.

CHOCOLATE-ORANGE MILKSHAKE CAKE

**MAKES TWO LAYERS OF
20-CM/8-INCH ROUND CAKE**

325 g/11½ oz/1½ cups soft
    brown sugar

175 g/6⅛ oz/¾ cup super-soft
    butter

125 ml/4½ fl oz/½ cup vegetable
    oil (or any other light oil)

120 g/4¼ oz/¾ cup milk or dark
    chocolate, melted

Zest of 1 orange (optional)

3–4 drops of orange essence
    (optional)

3 large eggs

150 ml/5¼ fl oz/⅔ cup soured
    cream, crème fraiche or
    plain yoghurt

400 g/14 oz/3¼ cups self-raising
    flour, sifted

30 g/1 oz/¼ cup cocoa powder

250 ml/8 fl oz/1 cup cold milk
    (full fat for indulgence,
    semi-skimmed, or even water,
    if you prefer)

This cake is ridiculously good, and it's one of our most popular wedding-cake choices at the bakery. It is deliciously indulgent – great for parties and celebrations, or just for a quiet weekend in . . . It's one of those cakes that you shouldn't really think too much about, forget about the calories and just enjoy!

Preheat your oven to 160°C/350°F/gas 4 and line two 20-cm/8-inch round baking tins with good-quality parchment.

In a large bowl, mix the sugar, butter and oil together until the mixture is as light and fluffy as you can get it. Then, pour in your melted chocolate and, if you like, add in the orange zest and essence here too, and mix again.

In a separate bowl, stir the eggs and soured cream together until you have a creamy-looking mixture with no lumps. Add this into your creamed butter/sugar mixture and stir until combined.

Tip in half of the self-raising flour and cocoa powder, then mix, then pour in half of the milk and mix again, using a whisk, if you need to, to make sure there are no lumpy bits. Then repeat, adding in the rest of the flour and cocoa powder, and the remaining milk, until you have a lush, thick milky batter.

Pour into your cake tins and bake for around 35–45 minutes, until a cocktail stick inserted into the cake comes out clean. Allow to cool before decorating (see pages 30–47 for frosting recipes).

FRUITY NUTTY CARROT CAKE

MAKES TWO 15- OR 18-CM/
6- OR 7-INCH ROUND CAKES

150 g/5¼ oz/⅔ cup butter, softened but not melted
150 g/5¼ oz/⅔ cup light soft brown sugar
1 tsp ground cinnamon
1 tsp ground ginger
Zest of 1 big orange
3 eggs
210 g/7½ oz/1⅔ cups self-raising wholemeal flour
A pinch of salt
90 g/3 oz/½ cup posh sultanas (flame yellow or
   California)/raisins/cranberries/blueberries
30 g/1 oz/¼ cup dried apricots, chopped
220 g/7¾ oz carrots (heritage purple ones are
   great), peeled and grated
80 g/2¾ oz/⅔ cup hazelnuts/pistachios/pecans,
   chopped
20 g/¾ oz/⅛ cup pumpkin seeds
   (or other seeds of your choosing)

According to something I read on the internet without any science behind it, carrots are one of those veggies that are "calorie neutral". Allegedly, they take so much flipping crunch and digestion energy that, by the time your body absorbs the calories from them, you've used them all up. Not that I trust internet-based nutritional quackery in any other area of my life, but if it gives me a reason to not feel guilty about eating lots of cake, I'm sold.

Preheat the oven to 180°C/400°F/gas 6. Line two 15- or 18-cm/ 6- or 7-inch baking tins with parchment paper.

In a food mixer (or roll your sleeves up!), beat the butter, sugar, spices, zest and eggs together until they are lighter in colour and have fluffed up in volume a bit.

Sift the flour into the eggy mixture and fold gently together, trying not to bash out the air bubbles too much.

Tip in your remaining ingredients and give a short mix to combine.

Pour into your baking tins and bake for around 25–30 minutes, until a cocktail stick inserted into the middle comes out just about clean (the mixture should still be a wee bit gooey).

This cake is great without any icing, but a slather of cream-cheese icing really brings it into the brilliant section!

BEETROOT AND CHOCOLATE CAKE

**MAKES TWO 15-CM/6-INCH ROUND CAKES
OR ONE 1-LB LOAF**

200 ml/7 fl oz/¾ cup vegetable
   or sunflower oil
240 g/8½ oz/1⅛ cups soft brown sugar
3 eggs
2 tsp vanilla-bean extract
200 g/7 oz/1½ cups self-raising flour
80 g/2¾ oz/⅔ cup cocoa powder
225 g/8 oz cooked beetroot, grated into strips as
   long as possible
100 g/3½ oz/⅔ cup milk chocolate, melted (or dark
   choc to make it dairy free)

I really love this recipe – it gives you a light chocolate sponge, with tasty soft flashes of grated beetroot throughout. Iced with a vanilla buttercream, or a slightly more savoury cream-cheese icing, it's the best.

As I've mentioned before, chocolate cake is really popular at Bee's Bakery for wedding cakes – we do one design that is very ivory and bridal looking from the outside, but when you cut into it, there's the beautiful contrast of the dark reddy-brown sponge against the white icing.

Preheat the oven to 170°C/375°F/gas 5 and line two 15-cm/6-inch baking tins or one 1-lb loaf tin with parchment.

Mix the vegetable oil, sugar and eggs together in a food mixer until they're light and fluffy and a little paler in colour – about 5 minutes.

Add in the vanilla extract, then the dry ingredients, and mix until combined.

Tip in the beetroot and melted chocolate at the end, and mix until combined – it will be a lumpy mixture.

Pour into your baking tins and bake for around 25 minutes – a cocktail stick, when inserted, will come out a little sticky still.

SUPERCOOL AUBERGINE CAKE

MAKES ONE 20-CM/8-INCH ROUND CAKE

200–250 g/7–8¾ oz (1 medium-sized) aubergine, cooked in the microwave (approx. 8 minutes) or roasted (20–30 minutes), cooled until warm, and skinned

300 g/10½ oz/2 cups milk or dark chocolate, finely chopped

3 eggs

180 g/6⅓ oz/1½ cups soft brown sugar

30 g/1 oz/¼ cup cocoa powder

80 g/2¾ oz/¾ cup self raising flour (subsitute gluten-free flour if required)

40 g/1½ oz/scant ½ cup ground almonds (or ground hazelnuts)

Well, well, well… this cake was a great surprise to me. In fact, I was working late one night, decorating a wedding cake, and I ate almost half of the test batch for this recipe with a spoon, straight out of the tin. Therefore, I can vouch for its super qualities – particularly in helping me ice a massive cake at 10 p.m.!

Vegetables such as aubergine, cauliflower and sweet potato work so well in baking because they add the bulk that's normally provided by the flour, but they also add some really interesting, deep, naturally good textures and tastes. For me, this makes baking interesting.

Preheat your oven to 160°C/350°F/gas 4 and line a 20-cm/8-inch baking tin with parchment.

A food mixer makes this recipe super fast, but if you prefer muscle power, that's possible too. Mash (by hand or mixer) the warm aubergine and finely chopped chocolate together until you have a sticky, smoothish goo – some lumps of chocolate are fine.

In a separate bowl, combine the eggs, sugar, cocoa powder, flour and ground almonds or hazelnuts, then add this to the chocolatey, auberginey mixture and pour into the baking tin.

Bake for 25–40 minutes, until a cocktail stick or skewer inserted comes out dry.

CHOCOLATE CAULIFLOWER CAKE

This is my idea of a really good "surprise inside" cake, and having taste-tested it on a few mates, it's quite hard to detect! It's a moist little cake, with more of a nutty flavour than anything else. The ground flaxseed here binds the mixture and helps the cake rise. Give it a whirl!

MAKES ONE 20-CM/8-INCH TRAY BAKE, OR 1-LB LOAF

250 g/8¾ oz defrosted, uncooked frozen cauliflower
1 tbsp vanilla-bean extract
3–4 tbsp vegetable oil
120 ml/4¼ fl oz/½ cup milk (cows' or soya works well, as does almond)
90 g/3 oz/⅔ cup wholemeal self-raising flour
25 g/1 oz/¼ cup cocoa powder
130 g/4½ oz ground flaxseed
130 g/4½ oz/½ cup soft brown sugar
150 g/5¼ oz/1 cup chocolate chips

Preheat your oven to 160°C/350°F/gas 4 and line a 20-cm/8-inch baking tray (or a 1-lb loaf tin) with parchment.

It's easiest to make this recipe with a food processor, so, first of all, blend the cauliflower, vanilla and vegetable oil until you have a smooth paste.

Then add in the milk and mix again.

Combine the flour, cocoa powder, flax and sugar in a separate bowl and pour into the wet mix, mixing on slow until combined. If you want to keep your choc chips whole, for a bit for a chocolatey bite when baked, add them right at the end.

Pour into your baking tin and bake for around 30–35 minutes, until a cocktail stick inserted comes out clean.

YOU SAY "COURGETTE", I SAY "ZUCCHINI" CAKE

I'm not a massive fan of courgettes, but my mum used to grow them in the garden when I was little, and I still remember her lovely courgette cakes. This isn't a bad way of sneaking a green veg into a little person's diet, and the cake is a lovely pale green speckledy colour when baked.

MAKES TWO 15-CM/6-INCH ROUND CAKES

2 tbsp chia seeds/poppy seeds/ millet/other small nutty seeds

200 g/7 oz/¾ cup vegetable margarine or very soft butter

200 g/7 oz/1 cup soft brown sugar

2 eggs

200 g/7 oz/1½ cups wholemeal self-raising flour

200 g/7 oz grated courgette (zucchini), skin and all

1 small red-skinned apple, grated

Zest of 2 limes

Preheat your oven to 160°C/350°F/gas 4 and line two 15-cm/ 6-inch baking tins with parchment.

Mix the seeds, margarine and brown sugar together in a bowl until the mixture is light and fluffy in texture.

Add in the eggs and mix again until combined, then add the flour and stir through.

Finally, add in the grated courgette, apple and lime zest, and mix until combined. Pour into the prepared tins.

Bake for 25–35 minutes, until a cocktail stick or skewer inserted comes out clean.

MY "ORANGE VEG IS OKAY" CAKE

MAKES ONE 15-CM/6-INCH ROUND CAKE

210 g/7½ oz/1 cup light or dark soft brown sugar
1–2 tsp ground cinnamon, to taste
1–2 tsp ground ginger, to taste
½ tsp ground cloves/allspice
3 eggs
200–250 g/7–8¾ oz cooked and puréed sweet potato/
    butternut squash/pumpkin
165 g/5¾ oz/1⅓ cups self-raising wholemeal flour

I find sweet potatoes and things like pumpkin quite confusing. I just don't get them! So I thought I'd try to understand them properly by putting them in a cake. It works, and it's tasty too! It's a bit like that famous coffee chain from the USA's pumpkin loaf cake, but minus about one thousand calories. And my in-laws didn't even notice there was a vegetable in the cake, so winner-winner, sweet-potato dinner.

Preheat your oven to 160°C/350°F/gas 4 and line a 15-cm/6-inch baking tin with parchment.

In a food mixer, beat the sugar, spices and eggs together until light and fluffy.

Add in about three-quarters of your puréed veggies and continue mixing until combined, then add the flour last of all. You're looking for a thick batter, here. If it's still quite runny, add in the rest of the puréed veg.

Spoon into your baking tin and bake for 25–40 minutes, until a cocktail stick or skewer inserted comes out dry.

SPICY JAMAICA GINGER CAKE

MAKES ONE 20-CM/8-INCH ROUND CAKE

225 g/8 oz/1¾ cups self-raising flour

1 tsp bicarbonate of soda

1 tsp ground cinnamon

1 tsp ground allspice

115 g/4 oz/½ cup butter, cold and diced

115 g/4 oz/⅓ cup black treacle/molasses

115 g/4 oz/⅓ cup golden syrup

115 g/4 oz/½ cup dark muscovado sugar

3–6 tbsp Jamaican ginger, peeled and grated, with the strings removed

275 ml/9⅔ fl oz/1⅛ cup full-fat dairy or non-dairy milk (soya works well)

1 egg

I spent the first few years of my time living in London staying in the north-east of the city, where my friend, Ohaji, introduced me to a knockout variety of fresh Jamaican ginger on the Ridley Road market in Dalston.

Jamaican ginger is smaller and knobblier than regular ginger, and packs an incredible punch, with a lovely depth of flavour, so it makes this ginger-cake recipe truly something else! If you can make the cake a couple of days before serving, it will reward you with an amazing sticky texture, and it is even more delicious when served with cool cream-cheese icing.

Preheat your oven to 180°C/400°F/gas 6 and line one 20-cm/8-inch round cake tin.

Sift the flour, bicarbonate of soda and spices (barring the grated ginger) into a large bowl – this seems like extra admin, but if you do the sifting twice, it adds a lovely lightness to the end cake.

Using your fingertips, rub the butter into the flour until you have fine breadcrumbs – try not to over-mix.

Gently heat the treacle, golden syrup, sugar and grated ginger in a small pan until a little melted, but not bubbling or boiling. Remove from the heat, then pour the milk on top and mix until combined. Pour this mixture on top of your flour/butter combo and mix well, adding the egg last of all.

Pour the mixture into your lined tin and bake for around 40–50 minutes, depending on the depth of the cake; you'll know it's ready when a cocktail stick inserted into the sponge comes out clean.

Store in an airtight container and, if you can, eat after a couple of days – it ages so well!

ICINGS AND ICING TECHNIQUES

VANILLA BUTTERCREAM

**MAKES ENOUGH TO FILL
ONE LAYER OF A 20-CM/
8-INCH SPONGE**

**FOR BIGGER QUANTITIES, JUST
MULTIPLY AWAY!**

150 g/5¼ oz/⅔ cup salted butter,
   softened but not melted
   (you can substitute vegetable
   margarine or vegan spread,
   if you like)
170 g/6 oz/1⅓ cups icing
   (powdered) sugar, sifted if
   there are any lumps
2 tsp vanilla-bean paste

A good, reliable buttercream is to baking what the colour black is to fashion – it goes with everything. This recipe is solid enough to use for a cake filling in a layer cake, to do a crumb coat and a final coat. It can be used to pipe the buttercream succulents and flowers on page 68 and the wedding cake on page 74. I've listed a few ideas for additions, but get creative and add your own twists too!

If you have a desktop or hand-held mixer, use it for this recipe – either that or face guaranteed baking biceps, as it'll take a lot of energy!

In a large bowl/the bowl of your mixer, slowly and gently combine the butter, icing sugar, vanilla and any flavours together. If you're doing this by hand, mix the icing sugar into the butter in thirds, otherwise it'll fly everywhere and create an icing-sugar storm in your kitchen. If you're using a mixer, place a clean tea towel over the bowl to stop the sugar storm.

When it's all combined and there are no lumps, this is the time to really give it a thrashing – whip the mixture around at full speed for at least 5 minutes by hand, or 3 minutes using the mixer. Scrape down the sides regularly, and keep going until the mixture is much paler in colour, and is light and fluffy in texture.

You can chill any leftover buttercream, just remember to remove it from the fridge an hour before you need it, and give it a nice energetic mix before using, to smooth any bubbles out.

Optional extras

○ Add in 2 tsp of lemon/orange/lime zest or be more adventurous and pick pink grapefruit, pomelo or a heritage citrus fruit zest.

○ Tear up brightly coloured edible petals and mix them through, for a pretty effect.

○ Pour in 3–4 drops of rosewater, or orange, almond or peppermint essence.

○ Add 1 tbsp of poppy seeds, for a cool speckled effect.

○ Soak some Earl Grey tea leaves in a little milk for an hour before adding, for a subtle tea-time taste.

○ Replace 25–35 g/about 1 oz/¼ cup of icing sugar with cocoa powder, for a simple chocolatey twist.

○ Add in 40 g/1½ oz/¼ cup melted chocolate for a really fancy-pants chocolate buttercream.

○ Add in 1 tbsp of freeze-dried fruit powders, such as raspberry, beetroot or blueberry, for a sharp flavour burst.

○ Be more adventurous and add in some bits with health benefits, e.g. matcha powder, spirulina or baobab fruit powder.

○ Add in a sprinkling of crushed rose petals or finely ground culinary lavender for a floral note.

○ Tear up 5–6 mint leaves or basil leaves and add alongside 1 tbsp of lemon zest, for a fancy herbal factor.

○ Add a shot of amaretto and some almond essence, for a boozy take.

ROYAL ICING

MAKES ENOUGH TO COVER A
20-CM/ 8-INCH CAKE, OR TO
ATTACH DECORATIONS TO AT
LEAST THE SAME SIZE OF CAKE

2 egg whites, or powdered egg
white (check the instructions
on the packet in case the
quantity of icing changes)
A squeeze of lemon juice – about
a quarter of a lemon's worth
(this stops the icing yellowing)
500 g/1 lb 1⅔ oz/4 cups icing
(powdered) sugar, sifted if
there are any lumps or clumps
Piping gel, as needed
(if you're planning on intricate
piping work, this stuff is a
good investment as it makes
the icing flow more easily –
optional)
Paste food colours (optional)

As well as being the perfect icing to use for decoration and piping work, royal icing is the edible glue of the cake world. There are two different consistencies that we use most regularly at Bee's Bakery and I've outlined how to make them below.

This is one recipe for which I'd definitely use a mixer, as it is really hard work to get a nice smooth stiff-peak icing otherwise – so, if you have one, go ahead and make it useful. Otherwise, flex your muscles and get ready for some real work, Arnie!

Pour your egg whites and lemon juice into a large bowl and give a little mix just to combine.

Tip in half of your sifted icing sugar and begin to mix gently. If you're using a mixer, then cover the open bowl with a clean tea towel to avoid the icing sugar flying all over the place!

Keep adding in the icing sugar until you have a super-thick, creamy and smooth mix – you do need to give it some welly, here, and keep scraping down the sides of the bowl to make sure it all combines. It'll look thick and glossy, but not wet, when it's done.

As royal icing will set hard if exposed to the air, I usually keep my icing in an airtight container and cover the top of the icing with a spanking new piece of jiffy cloth or several layers of kitchen towel dampened with water.

Consistencies

Stiff peak As per the above recipe; used to glue paper flowers on to cakes, or stick tiers to each other. This consistency is super-strong, but may vary according to the size of the egg whites used. Add more icing sugar if needed – you're looking for a super thick paste here.

Soft peak The above recipe with water added drop by drop and a teaspoon of piping gel stirred in, until a slightly softer icing is formed that still holds its shape. Used for piping detail or messages on top of cakes. When ribboned in the bowl, this icing trail will sink into the main pool of icing after around 10 seconds.

CHOCOLATE GANACHE

**MAKES ENOUGH ICING TO COVER
ONE 20-CM/8-INCH LAYER CAKE**

200 g dark or milk chocolate
200 ml/7 fl oz/¾ cup double
   cream
200 g/7 oz/1⅓ cups dark or
   milk chocolate

Wow – this stuff is lush, and will really elevate the taste and look of your cakes and bakes. It's easy to make and easy to store (in the fridge for a week, or the freezer for a month). Using it (especially in hot weather) takes a bit of getting used to, but it's also easy to "fix" – if it sets before you're finished working with it, just microwave for a few seconds to bring it back to glossy and workable. I tend to use a budget chocolate as the base, as adding the cream really jazzes up the quality, anyway.

Heat the double cream in a saucepan over a medium heat until it just gently comes to a simmer.

Meanwhile, chop up your chocolate into regularly sized small pieces and place these in a large bowl.

When the cream is ready, pour it on top of the chocolate pieces and scrape out the pan to make sure you have every drop of cream.

Mix gently with a whisk until you have a lovely, thick, shiny chocolate goo.

You can use this ganache in several ways
- As soon as it's melted, pour or drizzle it on top of your cake.

- Once it's cooled a little bit and thickened, use it to fill your cake or ice the outside, using a palette knife for a pretty-but-rough style icing finish.

- Once it's cooled all the way, use a piping bag to create piped swirls on top of your cake.

SWISS MERINGUE BUTTERCREAM

**MAKES ENOUGH TO FILL ONE
20-CM/8-INCH LAYER CAKE**

120 g/4¼ oz/½ cup caster
    (superfine) sugar
2 egg whites
250 g/8¾ oz/1⅛ cups butter,
    at room temperature and
    chopped into little chunks
1 tsp vanilla extract

This stuff is pure indulgence. It's super-soft, silky, absolutely, utterly delicious – and guaranteed to give you a baker's belly if consumed in large quantities! It really is the classiest icing you can get, and looks utterly gorgeous on cakes. However, it's a bit of a pain to make and work with, especially in warm weather, so I'd suggest only having a go once you consider yourself a bit of a pro with regular buttercream icing.

Warning: this recipe really does need a hand or stand mixer – it's really, really hard work without one!

Pour your caster sugar and egg whites into a bowl set over a pan of gently simmering water and whisk continuously until the sugar is totally melted into the egg white, which will be warm and frothy at this point. This should take a few minutes only, so shouldn't be bubbling hot. Test the sugar is melted by pinching a little of the mixture between two fingers – if it's grainy, keep mixing; once it's smooth, you can stop!

Transfer this mixture to the bowl of your stand mixer, or use a hand mixer. Use the whisk attachment to mix at high speed for around 3–4 minutes, until the mixture is super white in colour and forms stiff peaks, and the bowl is cool.

Turn the mixer to medium speed and add in your butter, a couple of small pieces at a time, waiting for each bit to be mixed in before adding more. Don't worry if your mixture looks like it has split at any point, just keep adding in the butter and it'll come back together.

Finally, add in your vanilla extract and use in the same way you'd use buttercream, bearing in mind that it's super buttery and therefore much more susceptible to heat than normal.

EASY-PEASY SUGAR-PASTE/ FONDANT ICING

MAKES ENOUGH ICING TO COVER A 20-CM/8-INCH LAYER CAKE

500 g/1 lb 1²/₃ oz large white
    marshmallows
1 tbsp water
1 tsp vanilla essence (optional)
Paste food colours (optional)
850 g–1 kg/1 lb 14 oz–2 lb 3¼ oz/
    6½–8 cups icing (powdered)
    sugar

At Bee's Bakery, we mostly use shop-bought, pre-made sugar-paste icing – but it can be expensive, and often contains animal-origin gelatin. If you want to avoid this, then making it at home is actually pretty easy, and satisfying too – if a wee bit messy!

If you fancy giving it a try, here's a recipe that uses marshmallows as the base – check the ingredients list on the packaging to make sure yours are vegetarian, if you need them to be.

Place your marshmallows and 1 tablespoon of water in a large microwave-safe bowl. Microwave on the high setting for 1–2 minutes, until the marshmallows start to melt and puff up a bit. Remove and stir in the water, then heat again for 30 seconds at a time, mixing in-between blasts, until you have a nice smooth consistency. Add the vanilla essence and a colour, if you'd like, at this point.

Now, using a wooden spoon or spatula, stir in about a quarter of the icing sugar at a time. You may need to knead in the last bit of icing sugar on a work surface – it'll be a pretty hard-work dough at this stage.

Wrap twice in cling film, if not using immediately, and when ready to use, roll out on to an icing-sugar-dusted work surface and use exactly as you would a ready-to-roll icing.

Additional technique – marbled sugar-paste icing
You can achieve a cool marbling effect by swirling and painting thin lines of paste food colouring over the surface of a piece of white sugar-paste icing, before kneading a tiny amount and rolling out on to a work surface dusted with icing sugar.

DAIRY-FREE VEGAN ICINGS

I've got a couple of friends with kids who are allergic to dairy … and I know it's hard to fake it sometimes, so here are two good vegan icing recipes for you, Kat! Matching the taste of full-fat, sugar-laden buttercream or cream-cheese icing just isn't possible without animal products, but if you want to give those a rest, these are good alternatives. Be careful which vegetable spread you choose, since some vegan spreads (e.g. soya spread) have added water, which makes for a really runny icing, which may curdle. I use sunflower or vegetable spread, mixed in with a white vegetable fat such as Trex or Crisco, and make sure I add in extra flavourings e.g. lemon zest, or a splash of good-quality vanilla, to improve the taste. Some grated dark chocolate (look for 0% milk solids in the ingredients) gives a lovely speckled finish and extra flavour too.

Use and serve these icings cold – it really makes a difference!

THESE RECIPES EACH MAKE ENOUGH TO FILL *OR* ICE A 20-CM/ 8-INCH CAKE

VEGAN BUTTERCREAM
250 g/8¾ oz/1 ⅛ cups vegetable spread or vegetable shortening
280–300 g/10–10½ oz/2¼–2⅓ cups icing (powdered) sugar, to taste (some vegan spreads have a higher water content than others, so you may need more)
2 tsp vanilla-bean extract
Zest of at least 1 lemon/lime

VEGAN CREAM CHEESE
250 g/8¾ oz/1⅛ cups vegan-branded cream cheese
100 g/3½ oz/½ cup vegetable spread or vegetable shortening
150–200 g/5¼–7 oz/1¼–1½ cups icing (powdered) sugar, to taste (some vegan spreads have a higher water content than others, so you may need more)
2 tsp vanilla-bean extract
Zest of 1 lemon

VEGAN BUTTERCREAM
Sift the icing sugar, if it's lumpy, and then, basically, just beat everything very well until combined and a little light and fluffy. If the icing is runny once mixed, add in a little more icing sugar.

VEGAN CREAM CHEESE
Beat everything very well until thoroughly mixed and a little light and fluffy.

TWO SUPER AVOCADO ICINGS

Avocados make great icing – who knew?! For a lovely, rich, cool green-coloured icing, have a go at the first recipe, but if the greenness is a bit of a fright for you first-timers, try the second recipe, with a chocolatey edge.

EACH RECIPE MAKES ENOUGH TO FILL *OR* ICE THE TOP OF ONE 15-CM/6-INCH CAKE

GREEN AVOCADO ICING
200 g/7 oz super-ripe avocados (around 2 big ones)
2 tbsp butter/non-dairy margarine
1 tsp vanilla-bean extract
A pinch of salt
400–450 g/14 oz–1 lb/3–3½ cups of icing (powdered) sugar (the amount depends on the consistency you like best)

CHOCOLATE AVOCADO ICING
100 g/3½ oz super-ripe avocado (around 1 whole one)
50 g/1¾ oz/⅓ cup cocoa powder
75–100 ml/2½–3½ fl oz/⅓–½ cup maple syrup (depends on the wetness of the avocado, and how sweet you like it)
40–50 g/1½–1¾ oz/¼–⅓ cup chocolate chips or chopped chocolate pieces for extra crunch

GREEN AVOCADO
It's easier to use a mixer or blender for this recipe, but there's also an argument for doing a bit of a workout before consuming it, so take your pick!

Mix, mash and purée the avocado and butter/margarine together in a large bowl, until you have a smooth green paste with no lumps.

Mix in the vanilla and salt, then pour in around half of the icing sugar.

Cream until combined, then add in the rest of the icing sugar and mix before assessing the consistency – is it too runny? If so, add in some more icing sugar.

Ice your cake and consume pretty sharpish, or store the icing in an airtight bag or Tupperware container for up to 3 days.

CHOCOLATE AVOCADO
This one is super easy. Throw everything into a blender and blitz until combined! Have a little taste; add more maple syrup if it's not sweet enough for you.

VEGAN CHOCOLATE AND CAULIFLOWER ICING

Alternatives to very fatty, high-dairy-content icings really float my boat – I'm not a one-hundred-per-cent health nut, but I do think that exploring alternatives in baking is creative, fun and quite delicious. I've blind taste-tested this recipe on a few friends, and no one can guess the vegetable! It has a great consistency, and it works out cheaper than regular buttercream, especially if you get hold of one of those whacking big bags of frozen cauliflower and keep it in the freezer.

MAKES ENOUGH TO FILL OR ICE ONE 20-CM/8-INCH LAYER CAKE

350 g/12⅓ oz cauliflower, fully cooked and cooled

2 tbsp lemon juice

120 ml/4¼ fl oz/½ cup coconut oil or mild vegetable oil (e.g. groundnut oil)

100 g/3½ oz avocado (around 1 large one)

200 ml/7 fl oz/¾ cup maple syrup (to taste)

100 g/3½ oz/¾ cup cocoa powder (or 40 g/1½ oz/⅓ cup raw cacao)

40 g/1½ oz/¼ cup dark chocolate (or more to taste if you like), melted

2 tsp vanilla-bean extract

A big pinch of salt

In a blender, purée the well cooked and cooled cauliflower along with the lemon juice, scraping down the sides and nooks and crannies of your food mixer, until you have a smooth, thick paste.

Add the oil and avocado, and purée again until as smooth as you can get it.

Add the syrup, cocoa, chocolate, vanilla and salt, and blend one last time for a couple of minutes, until creamy.

Refrigerate for at least 1 hour before using. Store any leftover icing in the freezer for up to 1 month.

DAIRY-FREE CASHEW-CREAM ICING

**MAKES ENOUGH ICING TO
EITHER FILL OR ICE ONE
20-CM/8-INCH LAYER CAKE**

120 g/4¼ oz/1 cup cashew nuts,
   soaked in water for at least
   2 hours, drained and rinsed
2 tbsp coconut oil
3 tbsp maple syrup (or honey,
   to taste)
A squeeze of lemon juice
A good pinch of salt
1 tsp vanilla-bean extract
1–3 tbsp non-dairy milk (e.g.
   almond, oat, soya), if needed

Despite running a commercial bakery for over three years now, I'm still learning. Whilst I'm not a vegan myself, I do have regular vegan days, and I think that tasting and trying different recipes, and learning about alternative ways to eat without consuming animal products, is one of the more innovative parts of baking these days.

This recipe for a nut-based icing is great, and there are tons of healthy fats in the nuts and coconut oil, which can't be anything but a winner! Don't forget to soak your cashews in advance, to make the icing super-smooth.

You really do need a blender for this recipe, as it's impossible to get the nuts puréed finely enough without it – a stick blender or probably something like a NutriBullet would work really well.

Blend just the cashew nuts by themselves for a couple of minutes, until smooth and as puréed/powdered as possible.

Add in the coconut oil, syrup/honey, lemon juice, salt and vanilla, and blend again to combine, scraping down the sides and prising out any trapped nuts from the blender bowl.

You are looking for a thick, creamy consistency, so you may need to add in a little non-dairy milk to loosen it up, but don't add too much – the thicker and creamier, the better, as it'll stick to your cake more easily.

Transfer to a bowl or Tupperware container and chill overnight or freeze for an hour, after which time the icing will have thickened and will be easier to work with.

PEANUT BUTTER ICING

MAKES ENOUGH TO FILL OR ICE THE TOP OF ONE 15-CM/ 6-INCH CAKE

220 g/7¾ oz/1 cup peanut butter (crunchy or smooth – your choice!)

120 g/4¼ oz/½ cup non-dairy (e.g. soya, vegetable) margarine

210 g/7½ oz/1 ⅔ cups icing (powdered) sugar, sifted, if it's lumpy

1 tsp vanilla-bean extract

2–4 tbsp non-dairy milk (soya works well in this one, but almond would also be good)

OMG! This icing is seriously addictive – you have been warned! Go easy with this stuff – it's super indulgent.

In a large bowl, using your bicep power, mix together the peanut butter and margarine until they have a smooth consistency, with no lumpy bumpy bits.

Add in the sifted icing sugar, vanilla and 2 tbsp of the soya milk, then mix to combine. You're looking for a nice thick, glossy consistency, so you may need to add a little more soya milk to achieve this.

Store in a covered bowl or Tupperware container for 1 hour before using, or freeze any leftovers for up to one month.

HOME-MADE SPRINKLES

You will need

A clean baking tray (or three)

Good-quality parchment paper
  or a silicon baking mat

1 x batch of royal icing
  (see page 34)

Several small bowls

Different paste food colourings

Several piping bags

Posh number 2 piping nozzles
  (optional)

This is possibly *the* most satisfying decorating recipe to make – especially the smashing-up part! It also comes with a guaranteed "Oh, *that's* how they do it" factor. They are a ton of fun and so, so easy and super personalizable, you'll definitely have a blast making your own. You can use them on cakes, cookies, on ice cream and puddings, or give as gifts in little jars ... They're ace.

It is a "leave overnight" type of recipe, so factor this into your planning.

Line a couple of baking trays with good-quality parchment or a silicon mat.

Prepare the royal icing to a piping consistency – it needs to be smooth and silky and hold its shape when ribboned, without being too runny. Divide it up into small bowls and mix the colours you'd like for your sprinkles. I went all out and made red, turquoise, orange, white, purple, green, pink and yellow. You can make them as pastel or bright as you like with these – they all look ace! If there's a gap between making and piping, cover the bowls with damp j-cloths or kitchen roll while you do this, so the icing doesn't start to harden.

If you want to have super-slick, professional-looking sprinkles, use a number 2 piping nozzle, and pipe long straight lines the length of the tray. I secure the top of the piping bag before I start, by folding the top down, or using one of those little bag-clasp thingies; you should always do this when piping, as it helps to stop the icing squishing out of the top of the piping bag.

My tip for getting straight lines is to hold the piping bag in your dominant hand and touch the piping nozzle with the index finger of your other hand. This gives you a little "push and pull" control of the direction of the nozzle. I also recommend you start piping at the furthest end of the baking tray, and pull the line of icing towards you, to help you get a straight line. (There's nothing wrong with wiggly lines at all, so don't worry too much if the line goes wonky!)

Once you have piped all of your colours, allow the icing to dry overnight before gently breaking up the strands into the size and shape you like best. If you're in a super hurry, you could put the trays into a cool oven (max 50°C/120°F) for about 45 minutes to speed up the drying process.

Store your home-made sprinkles in a jar or airtight container for up to a month.

HOW TO ICE A CAKE

HOW TO APPLY A CRUMB COAT

A crumb coat is a light coating of icing, that seals the crumbs to the cake before a second layer is added. This first coat is chilled before the next, thicker layer is added. Its not essential to crumb coat your cakes, but it does help to create a neater finish to a fully decorated cake. You can also use it to cover any blemishes, e.g. little holes in the cake, so that you have a lovely even, smooth base layer upon which to ice the final coat.

To apply a crumb coat, spoon a couple of dollops of icing onto the top of your layered cake and, using a palette knife and side scraper (if you have one), smooth a really thin layer of icing all the way over the cake, scraping the icing on, and off again, so that you can still see some of the cake through it, to avoid wastage. Imagine that you're creating the perfect cake shape, so if your side is a little wonky, build up the icing to make it appear straight. Fill in any little holes, and finish off with some lovely sharp edges.

HOW TO COVER A CAKE WITH SUGAR PASTE

On a clean worksurface dusted with icing sugar or cornflour, roll out your sugar paste to around 2 cm/¾ inch thick, lifting and turning it as you roll to make sure it's nice and even all over. How much icing you need depends on the diameter and height of the cake, but as a general guide, around 1 kg/2¼ lb of sugar paste should cover a 20-cm/8-inch round cake. Once you have a nice large circle of sugar paste, tuck and roll the piece back over the rolling pin and carefully lay it over the cake, making sure that the icing completely covers the cake, like a blanket. Straight away, tuck the edges of the sugar paste into the bottom of the cake to prevent the weight of the icing pulling the edges down and causing cracks or tears in the icing. If this happens, re-roll the icing a little thicker and have another go!

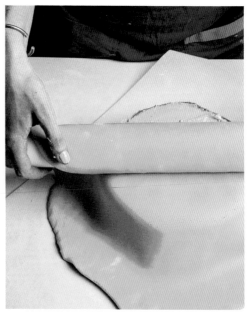

HOW TO SMOOTH ICING

Using a pair of cake smoothers (or the clean, icing-sugar-dusted palms of your hands) to create a smart, smooth, bump-free finish on sugar-paste-iced cakes. Once the sugar paste has been applied to the cake, gently run your hands all over the cake, tucking in any loose edges and making sure the icing is stuck to the cake all over. Then, using a knife or the edge of your cake smoother, press down on the edge of the icing that touches the work surface, and gently trim off any excess icing, saving it for another time. Run the cake smoothers all over the cake, using gentle pressure to smooth out any lumps or bumps. Work with one cake smoother on top, and one around the side, using a slight see-saw motion to create smart straight sides. Slide the side smoother upwards, from bottom to top, whilst moving the other smoother from the middle to the outside edge of the cake, to create lovely sharp edges. If you have air bubbles in the icing, prick these with a clean pin, and smooth over the top. Finish off your bottom edge with a length of ribbon, which can hide any scuff marks or a slightly wonky edge.

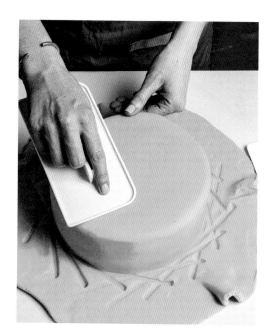

CAKE PROJECTS

VEGAN BANANA DRIP CAKE

MAKES TWO 20-CM/8-INCH ROUND CAKES

For the banana cake

8 very ripe and blackened medium-sized bananas

350 g/12¼ oz/1¾ cup soft brown sugar

120 ml/4¼ fl oz/½ cup vegetable oil

2 tsp vanilla-bean extract

375 g/13 oz/3 cups self-raising flour

A large pinch of salt

For the vegan buttercream

500 g/1 lb 1⅔ oz/2¼ cups soft, non-dairy spread (or vegetable margarine)

600 g/1 lb 5 oz/4¾ cups icing (powdered) sugar

1–2 tsp vanilla-bean extract

⅓ tsp yellow paste/gel food colouring (use a vegan brand)

For the sugar-paste icing

1 kg/2 lb 3¼ oz white sugar-paste icing (see page 37 and use vegan marshmallows)

Yellow paste/gel food colouring (use a vegan brand)

For the drizzle

200 g/7 oz/1⅓ cups dark chocolate (check it does not contain milk solids)

1 tbsp olive oil

This recipe is in my top three most-ordered cakes at Bee's Bakery; it is honestly one of the best, and when we get an order in for it, I always accidentally on purpose make way too much batter. You really need super-duper, almost grossly overripe bananas for this recipe. At the bakery, we stockpile our bashed bananas and freeze them, then defrost overnight before baking. They look really slimy and grim, but they make for the most delicious cake of all – I promise!

Dehydrated fruits also rock my world . . . The food colouring is optional, but it can add an amazing intensity to the fruits, making them look so pretty, fun and mad-looking, all at the same time, and they're extra easy to make ... You need to prepare these the night before you need them – see method on page 53.

You will need two cake smoothers, or icing paddles, for this recipe – these are flat-sided plastic paddles which, when used on the sides and top of the cake, create a lovely smooth finish to sugar-paste icing. You can just use your hands, if you like, but it'll be more tricky to achieve a lovely straight edge. You'll also need a squeezy bottle for applying the drizzle; an empty, clean squeezy ketchup bottle or even a fine-lipped jug would also do the trick.

For the cake

Preheat your oven to 160°C/350°F/gas 4, and line two 20-cm/8-inch round baking tins with good-quality parchment paper.

Mash, beat and whisk your bananas together with the sugar, until they are smooth with absolutely no lumps, lighter in colour and a little bubbly in texture – this should take about 10 minutes by bicep, or 5 minutes in a food mixer. Add the vegetable oil and vanilla, and beat until well combined.

Next, add in the flour and salt, and mix until combined, ensuring no lumps.

Pour your mixture into the tins, spreading the mixture evenly, all the way to the edges, and make a slight well in the middle to ensure the cake rises evenly.

Bake for around 30–35 minutes, until a skewer comes out clean and the sponge bounces back when pressed.

≫

Meanwhile, prepare your buttercream by mixing all the ingredients well, until light and fluffy and you have your desired strength of yellow colour. Some vegan margarines are a little "wet", so try mixing two types, and adding in some extra icing sugar, if this happens.

When cool, remove the cakes from the tin, trim off any knobbly bits so the tops are nice and flat, then layer them up with a thin layer of buttercream. Once you've stacked the layers up, crumb coat the cake (see page 46) and place in the fridge to chill for 1 hour.

Meanwhile, colour your sugar-paste icing using a small amount of paste colouring. Add a few splashes of water and knead well if it starts to crack, and wrap well in cling film until you're ready to use.

Once the cake has chilled, roll out your sugar paste on a worktop dusted with cornflour, to around 2 cm thick. Follow the instructions on page 46 to cover the cake in the sugar paste and smooth it out to nice sharp edges.

Allow the cake to rest whilst you prepare the chocolate drizzle.

Melt your chocolate gently, either in a bain-marie or in the microwave, adding the olive oil when done, and mix until glossy.

To achieve the upside-down drips, gently flip the cake upside down on to a baking sheet lined with parchment paper. Using a squeezy bottle or a fine-lipped jug, gently and slowly pour the chocolate around the top edge of the cake (which will become the bottom edge of the finished cake), allowing drips to fall over the side. Control how much the chocolate flows carefully to achieve varying thickness and length of drips. Allow the drips to set hard (sometimes I put the cake into the freezer for a few minutes) before flipping the cake back the right way up, and then drizzle around the top edge, as before.

Decorate using your thin slices of dehydrated fruit by pressing one edge gently into the icing, and using dots of buttercream, as needed, to support their weight.

DEHYDRATED FRUIT DECORATIONS

Around 20 pieces of dehydrated fruit slices
(I used kiwis, nectarines, pears, apples,
dragon fruit and strawberries)
Paste/gel food colours in your favourite bright tones
(use vegan brands)

Prepare your dehydrated fruits the night before you need them. Slice the fruits as thinly as possible. If desired, dip them in the edible food dyes (paste food colours mixed with a little water). Dehydrate for 6–8 hours, or overnight, at around 40°C.

I have a snazzy dehydrating machine. I say snazzy ... I mean cheap, but it's amazing and does a really great job. If you're not in the market for filling your home with appliances, you can use your home oven at its lowest setting (40–50°C/100–120°F/gas ¼), with the door slightly ajar to let the steam out.

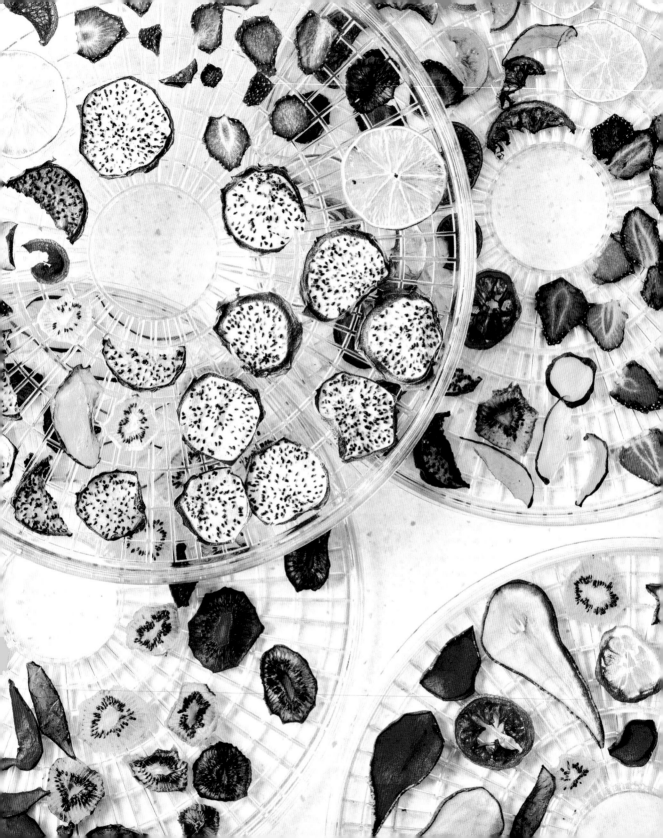

VERTICALLY STRIPED CHOCOLATE BIRTHDAY CAKE WITH MATCHA BUTTERCREAM

MAKES ONE 20-CM/8-INCH
ROUND CAKE
(ALTHOUGH IT DEPENDS ON THE
THICKNESS OF SPONGE BAKED)

For the sponge
12 eggs
350 g/12⅓ oz/1⅔ cups light soft
    brown sugar
1 tbsp good-quality vanilla-bean
    extract
180 g/6⅓ oz/1½ cups self-raising
    flour
100 g/3½ oz/¾ cup cocoa powder
75 g/2⅔ oz/¾ cup ground
    almonds
120 g/4 ¼ oz/½ cup butter,
    melted

For the matcha buttercream
500 g/1 lb 1⅔ oz/2¼ cups butter,
    at room temperature
2 heaped tbsp matcha powder
600 g/1 lb 5 oz/4¾ cups icing
    (powdered) sugar

I love this cake, with its vertical stripes! It's a hidden-construction gem, and so satisfying when someone cuts into it and says, 'Ooooh, how did you do that?!'

The balloons were made by my brilliant prop stylist and friend, Charlie Philips, who I worked with on my first book, *Bee's Brilliant Biscuits*, and this one too. They're so funny and little and perky – the perfect DIY topper, in my opinion.

Preheat your oven to 160°C/350°F/gas 4, and line 2 large baking trays, each a minimum of 25 cm/10 inches across and 30 cm/12 inches long, with good-quality parchment paper. For this type of cake, I use a really cool, foil-lined parchment paper that is extra strong.

Whisk your eggs, sugar and vanilla-bean extract together until bubbly, foamy and light in texture – this should take 5–8 minutes in a mixer, or 10 minutes by bicep power.

Next, fold in the flour, cocoa powder and ground almonds, mixing well to ensure there are no lumps.

Add in the butter, mix until combined, then pour into your two baking trays – you want the mix to be around 2–3 cm/1 inch in height all over, so spread the mixture evenly, all the way to the edges, and make a slight well in the middle to ensure the sponge layer bakes evenly. The sponge you are looking for here is ideally 2 cm thick, if it's any thicker it may crack when rolled.

Bake for around 10–12 minutes, until a skewer comes out clean and the sponge bounces back when pressed – it's a really bouncy sponge, this one.

⊳⊳

As soon as it's baked, whilst still hot, trim each sponge into two strips with a pair of scissors – approximately 14 cm/5 inches across and as long as the tin – cutting through the parchment paper as well as the cake. You might need to trim off some of the edges of the cake if they're crispy or cracking at all, and, if so, make sure your slabs of sponges are the same width (the length doesn't matter as much).

Whilst the sponge is warm, and leaving the parchment in place, roll each one into a spiral, gently but firmly, and place on its end to allow to cool for around 15–20 minutes.

Meanwhile, prepare your buttercream by beating all the ingredients together in a large bowl for at least 5 minutes, until light and fluffy and bright green in colour. The strength of matcha powders often varies, so if you're looking for a deeper colour, check that the taste isn't overpowering, and add a little more powder if you like.

Unravel one of the sponge rolls partially, peeling away the parchment gently as you go – this will form your central roll, so try to keep the spiral tight. You need just enough room to use a little palette or butter knife to spread the inside evenly with matcha buttercream. Once you've applied the buttercream, roll the central sponge up again tightly. For the next layer, unravel slightly and apply buttercream in the same way, but this time attach the start of this new roll to the end of your central spiral and wrap it aound, squeezing gently to seal it in shape. Repeat with one or two more rolls (you may not need them all - if not , see pages 126–129 for ideas to recycle the scraps), tucking the joins in firmly to seal the spiral with buttercream.

Crumb coat the cake, adding extra buttercream to even out the join at the end of the spiral, and place in the fridge to chill for 30 minutes.

Ice the cake in your preferred style. For this one, I applied a thick layer of matcha buttercream and then used the back of a teaspoon to drag the icing upwards in vertical stripes. The mini balloons tied on to cocktail sticks to make toppers create a party vibe!

FAVOURITE CEREAL CAKE - AKA THE CHEAT'S CAKE!

You will need

A layered cake, rough-iced with
   buttercream; it doesn't need
   to be chilled (I used a 3-layer
   Victoria sponge cake, filled with
   vanilla buttercream, jam, and
   iced with more buttercream)
Cereal shapes of your choosing –
   around half a box for a 20-cm/
   8-inch cake (I used Froot Loops)

Need a cake in a hurry? One that looks fun, but doesn't take too long to decorate? This is it: the ultimate cheat's cake.

Any cake will do (maybe even a shop-bought one – what am I saying?!), and any cereal with a regular shape will do too ... Imagine a Coco Pops cake, a Cheerios cake, a Honey Monster Puffs cake, a Nesquik cake ... The cake just needs to have a thin layer of buttercream or ganache on the outside, to give the cereal something to stick to.

Basically, all you need to do is press the cereal pieces gently on to the buttercream to stick them on.

If you fancy making a pattern, start on the top of the cake, working from the outside in, and then the top of the sides, working downwards in straight lines.

One thing to bear in mind is that the cereal will absorb the moisture from the buttercream, so it will go a bit chewy if left overnight ... Might as well finish the whole thing up, then!

MOTHERS' DAY SPLATTER CAKE

You will need

A cake of your choosing, iced with buttercream or sugar-paste/fondant icing in a pastel colour, with nice sharp edges

Small bowls or glasses to mix colours in

Cornflour or cocoa powder

Gel paste food colours (I used Sugarflair Fuschia, Royal Blue, Melon and Mint Green)

A pastry brush

Splatter cakes are a real "trick up your sleeve" – they look super effective, and are pretty easy to have fun with. It's such a quick technique and can transform a plain iced cake (buttercream or sugar paste) into something jazzy, cool, party-worthy and fun!

You can use a mixture of cocoa powder and a little water to make a cool chocolatey splatter, or paste food colours if you prefer the more colourful look. Drips and drizzles also look great, so it's worth experimenting with different thicknesses.

I started with a 3-layer cake at 20-cm/8-inches round, layered and iced with sugar-paste/fondant icing in a nice pale pink, then allowed to dry for a couple of hours before getting my splatter on.

Protect any work surfaces/clothes/the wall before you start – this stuff can get everywhere!

Into several small bowls, mix your chosen colours by stirring together around 2 tsp water, 1 tsp cornflour and a small amount of gel paste colour. The consistency you're looking for is quite thick, but cornflour does funny things, going hard and powdery if it's too thick, so be prepared to add in a few more drops of water/a bit of extra cornflour, as needed. You can get as creative as you like with colour, using pastels, or super brights – whatever you like!

Before starting on your cake, test out your flicking/splattering skills on a piece of parchment paper first. Dip the brush in a colour, then, holding the pastry brush in one hand, gently flick the bristles with the index finger of your other hand. Try loading up your brush more and then less, to achieve larger and smaller splatters, dots and drizzles. If you want thicker/larger drizzles, add more water and cornflour, and use a larger pastry brush.

Now you're ready to go wild on your cake! Start on the sides first, and remember – more is more, in this case. Leave to dry before serving.

To finish off the cake in true party style, add glittery cake toppers (see page 136).

GORGEOUS SUGAR-FLOWER BIRTHDAY CAKE

You will need

A layered and iced cake
(I used a 3-layer, 13-cm/
5-inch round sponge cake,
filled with vanilla buttercream
and raspberry jam,
crumb-coated with
buttercream and iced in
a pale yellow sugar paste)

Some edible gold spray paint

Flower paste (you can make your
own by adding gum tragacanth
to regular sugar paste)

Paste food colours (I used yellow,
baby blue and hot pink)

White vegetable fat or coconut oil

Piping gel / edible glue

Royal icing

A few cocktail sticks

A hard, smooth-surfaced plastic
chopping board or plastic mat

A silicone/plastic rolling pin

Flower- or petal-shaped sugar
paste cutters of your choice
(a company called JEM Cutters
sells a starter kit with about
30 of the most popular/useful
cutters in it, but you can also
buy individual little cutters)

A fine-pointed knife

A small, soft foam mat

A veining tool

A balling tool (looks a little like a
clay-modelling tool)

Making sugar flowers is a skill that's undergoing an increase in popularity, and there are some incredible artists to follow on Instagram. It's a tricky technique and one that you do need to invest a few quid into, to get the right starting kit, but once you've mastered the basics, you can get really creative. I first learned to make sugar flowers at night school in a posh borough of London at the "ladies' college", commuting home on my Vespa afterwards to my far less salubrious borough with carefully packed boxes of pretty sugar blooms.

The decorative elements of this cake will work with any base sponge in any size, so feel free to choose whatever you like.

To lustre the cake

To achieve the gold finish, spray-paint the surface of the sugar-paste icing with edible gold spray paint, from a distance of around 8–10 cm/4 inches. Follow the instructions on the can. My general tip is to avoid breathing in, and to aim for around 2–3 light coats of spray, allowing for drying time in between each one, to give an even finish.

To make the sugar flowers

It's important to think about how many flowers you want to make, how many petals (there are 5 here), the final size of the flowers, and guesstimate how large a centre you'll need to wrap your petals around.

Make your flower centres first. Depending on how many you need, take some flower paste and rub in a tiny amount of paste colour to create a shade you like (I used yellow). Use a cocktail stick to take a tiny amount out of the pot; a little goes a really long way. Once you are happy with the colour, break off small, similarly sized amounts of the flower paste and gently shape with your fingertips to form even round shapes, slightly flattening them. Allow to set a little.

Colour the flower paste for the petals in the same way. I separated the paste into 3 batches, colouring one pink, one blue and leaving one white.

⤏⤏

Smooth a very thin layer of white vegetable fat over the surface of your hard cutting board, using your fingertips. Then, with the rolling pin, roll out the petal flower paste to as thin as you can get it. Start by aiming for around 2 mm thick, and cut a petal out to see whether you can handle it gently without breaking it, then go thinner if you can. Gently press your cutter into the icing, then, using your fine-pointed knife, lift the petal off the board and on to the foam mat for shaping/veining. I used a medium-sized JEM round-petal cutter for this flower shape, but there are tons of options, here. You'll need around 5 petals per flower.

If you're going back and forth between cutting then shaping petals, it's a good idea to cover the exposed flower paste with cling film, as it sets hard quite fast and is really tricky to work with once it's all crunchy.

To vein the petal, gently roll the veining tool across the petal – doing this on the soft mat gives a more subtle effect, and on the hard mat a more pronounced one.

To soften the edges and create a more realistic petal effect, run the larger of the two balls on your ball tool around the edge of the petal. There is no real correct way to do this, so have a play; the harder you press, the more frilly the edge will become, and it may even tear a little, which is actually quite a realistic effect.

After shaping the petals, but before they set, apply a little edible glue/piping gel around the bottom "V" part of your first petal, and gently attach this to the centre ball you made earlier. It can be quite tricky to keep the centre ball in the middle of the overall flower shape once you start adding petals, so make sure it's positioned nice and centrally before you add the rest of the petals.

Using the same technique, add the other 4 petals to the flower, tucking one side of each petal underneath the petal preceding it, to give a realistic effect.

Rest your completed flower on some kitchen roll, perhaps tucked into an empty egg box to accentuate the flower shape, if you like. Allow the flowers to dry for at least 4 hours before attaching to the cake.

To attach the flowers to the cake, mix up some super-thick royal icing using the recipe on page 34 and pop it into a piping bag with a 1-cm hole cut into the end. Squeeze a generous amount on to the cake where you would like to position your flower, and gently press the flower into the icing, holding it in place to set for a few moments. To create extra height, you can make little round nuggets of sugar paste, and use them as plinths to raise the height of the flowers.

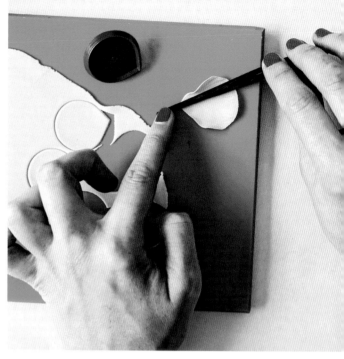

HAND-PIPED BUTTERCREAM FLOWERS AND SUCCULENTS

You will need

Cake or cakes, already crumb-coated (see page 46) and chilled (I used a 4-layer, 15-cm/6-inch beetroot and chocolate cake, iced with vanilla buttercream and a 3-layer, 13-cm/5-inch version of the same)

A flower piping nail

Good-quality parchment paper

Buttercream icing in your chosen colours (I used fuchsia pink, Christmas red, egg yellow, spruce green and holly green with a touch of midnight black)

Fabric piping bags and plastic couplers (optional; these allow you to switch piping nozzles without having to transfer icing to new bags)

Piping nozzles:

For the mini rose: a mini closed-star nozzle

For the ranunculus: Wilton nozzle 104 or a teardrop-shaped nozzle

For the dark green succulent: an upside-down rose tip, or a Wilton 150 nozzle

For the leafy succulent: a leaf-shaped nozzle

For the succulent with the "fingers": a number 4 or 6 round-tipped nozzle

Contrary to popular belief, hand-piping flowers and patterns on cakes didn't go out of fashion in the eighties, it's just that most of the textbooks are so old skool that they're off-putting! There are tons of ways to use classic hand-piping techniques to achieve a really cool, modern cake-decorating style.

I first studied cake decorating quite a few years ago at the Hampstead Garden Suburb Institute (yes, it was as clichéd as you can imagine), but I loved it, and I learned how to pipe buttercream roses there. I was recently asked to make a terrarium-themed birthday cake, and this planted a seed of inspiration.

This is a tricky technique to master, and it does need practice, but don't give up, because it is mega-satisfying when you get the knack of it ...

To prepare the cake, you will need

A palette knife

A side scraper (I used patterned ones with a small jagged-tooth finish)

To ice the cake

When you're ready to ice, place the cake/s directly on a clean work surface. Next, apply a thick layer of buttercream and, holding your side scraper at right angles, resting it on the work surface to get a nice sharp, straight edge, drag it cleanly across and around the surface of the cake/s, in one smooth motion (may take practice!). You will end up scraping quite a bit of icing off the cake/s, here.

Chill the cake/s again, before attaching the hand-piped flowers. To do this, simply dot a small amount of buttercream on to the cake/s and gently (but very quickly to avoid the icing melting) press each individual flower to stick.

To pipe the flowers

Before you add the buttercream to your piping bags, give it one last mix with your palette knife to knock any air bubbles out of the mix – this makes your petals look really smooth and professional.

⊅⊅

To pipe the larger rose shape

Attach a piece of parchment paper to the flower nail with a tiny dot of buttercream, and fill the piping bag, fitted with a Wilton nozzle 104 or another similar teardrop-shaped nozzle, with your favourite-coloured buttercream. Note: I used a pale pink buttercream, with a streak of dark pink painted down one side of the piping bag, to achieve the tinted-edge rose petals.

Start by piping a small, tight cone-shape in the centre of the piece of parchment – hold the flower nail in your less dominant hand, and spin it whilst you pipe with your dominant hand, touching the widest part of the piping nozzle to the flower nail.

Next, holding the piping nozzle at around a 45° angle to the centre cone, pipe three miniature rainbow shapes – these will make your first three petals around the middle cone you've created – tucking the end of each rainbow underneath the start of the next one and twisting the flower nail with your less dominant hand as you go – easier than it sounds! Try to pipe them really close to the central cone, so that it looks like the centre of a rose. If you get it wrong, no bother – scrape the buttercream off your parchment square, plop it back in the bowl and start again!

Next, pipe another three rainbow shapes around the outside, again tucking each of the ends of the petals underneath the next, but leaving a little of the centre cone and the first set of petals exposed.

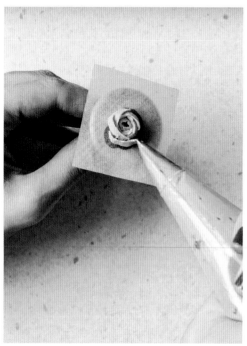

Try piping a little faster or a little slower; you'll find that different speeds/techniques result in different petal shapes – some with thinner petal edges, some with fatter ones. The angle at which you hold your piping bag will also determine how open the rose looks, so play around with different angles for different effects.

Depending on the size of your nozzle and centre cone, your next layer should need 5 petals to get all the way around the centre. Natural roses grow petals in odd numbers, so if you stick to this number scheme too, your piped rose will look more natural!

⊳⊳

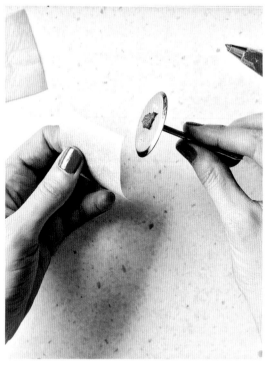

Keep piping until you have the size of rose you want. If there are any little lumps or bumps at the end, you can always cover these up with little leaves or other flowers.

Try to calculate the number of roses you'll need for your cake, and make a range of sizes – some tiny little buds and some larger open roses too – for variety.

Transfer your completed rose to a baking tray and freeze or chill very well before use.

To pipe the mini-rose shape

Place your pieces of parchment on to a flat surface and, using a mini closed-star nozzle, pipe several small dots of icing, about 1cm tall to act as a base – leave 2 cm in between each one.

Now, with an index finger guiding the nozzle of your piping bag if necessary, pipe a little spiral around each centre dot of icing, applying even pressure as you pipe and keeping as close to the central dot as possible. You should aim to loop around twice. Ease off on the pressure, and pull up and away quickly to finish the shape. You might want to tuck the "tail" of the icing in a little, to create a round shape.

Transfer to a baking tray and freeze or chill very well before use.

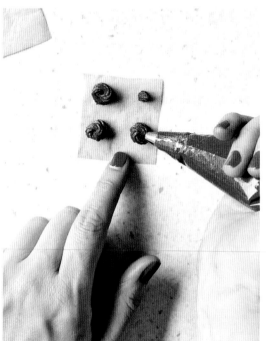

To pipe the leafy succulent

Attach a piece of parchment paper to a flower nail with a tiny dot of buttercream. Use a leaf-shaped nozzle and begin by piping a circle of leaf shapes around the outside of your parchment paper. Pipe this shape by applying strong pressure as you touch the nozzle to the paper, then quite quickly easing off and pulling away to create the tip of the leaf.

Pipe another circle of leaves inside the first one, and keep piping in this way, reducing the size slightly with each circle, until they join up in the middle and any gaps are filled in so that the succulent can be removed from the paper in one piece. Transfer to a baking tray and freeze or chill very well before use.

For the succulent with the "finger" shape

Using a similar technique to that used for the leafy succulent, pipe nice fat mini fingers (a round-tipped nozzle, size 4 or 6 works well for this) in a circle around the edge of your parchment square, all pointing towards the middle of the circle, but not touching; this allows for a flatter overall shape.

Repeat with another circle of finger shapes, in between the fingers of the first set, and continue until you reach the middle. Transfer to a baking tray and freeze or chill very well before use.

To pipe the dark-green succulent shape

Attach a piece of parchment paper to the flower nail with a tiny dot of buttercream, and fill the piping bag, fitted with a Wilton nozzle 150 or 104, or another similar-shaped nozzle with two rounded, more open edges, with your choice of green-coloured buttercream icing.

Start by piping a small cone in the centre of your parchment.

Next, turn the nozzle on its head, so the more open end is at the top. Again, as you would for the rose shape, pipe three petals around the outside of the centre cone, but this time keep the angle of the nozzle almost vertical, so that the succulent leaves end up being piped at a more upright angle – try for a slightly longer leaf shape than the classic rose shape.

Remember to tuck the end of each petal / leaf underneath the start of the next. Repeat by piping leaves in odd numbers around the centre, until you have a nice wide succulent shape. Aim for succulents in a few different shapes.

Transfer your finished succulents to a baking tray and freeze or chill really well before use.

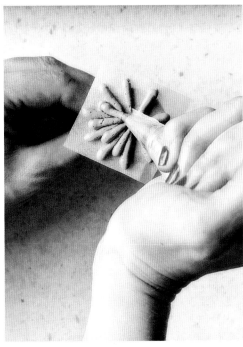

TIERED FLOWERFETTI LEMON AND LAVENDER WEDDING CAKE

MAKES A 3-TIERED CAKE, WITH THE TIERS SIZED 10, 15 AND 20 CM/4, 6 AND 8 INCHES

For the sponge
675 g/1 lb 7¾ oz/3 cups butter, very soft, but not melted

675 g/1 lb 7¾ oz/5 cups self-raising flour, sifted

12 eggs

675 g/1 lb 7¾ oz/3⅓ cups caster (superfine) sugar

1–2 heaped tbsp lavender buds (culinary-grade), very finely chopped

Zest of 3–4 lemons

Dash of lemon extract, to taste

1 tbsp vanilla-bean extract

For the buttercream
1 kg/2 lb 3¼ oz/4½ cups butter, at room temperature

1.2 kg/2 lb 10⅓ oz/8 cups icing (powdered) sugar, sifted

Zest of 2 lemons (or more, to taste)

1 generous tbsp vanilla-bean extract

For the decoration
4–5 punnets of edible flowers of your choosing (mine are from Maddocks Farm Organics – see stockists, page 144, for details)

Edible gold leaf

I adore making wedding cakes; it honestly rocks my world. Being asked into a couple's life to help them celebrate something beautiful, and knowing that what you bake will have a central part to play in a brilliant party – what could be better? I've also noticed how trends in the recipes that couples choose have changed in the last couple of years, with floral, citrusy, fresh recipes becoming favourites, rather than the more traditional Victoria sponges or fruit cakes.

I was first asked to make a "flowerfetti" cake in 2013, by Sabrina and James, for a supercool wedding in north London. I found the different varieties of edible petals available so inspiring that I decided to design a range of cakes based on it – and look where I am now! This recipe is dedicated to you, Sabrina – thank you!

You will need 3 round cake boards, sized at 10, 15 and 20 cm/4, 6 and 8 inches. Before you start, make sure the butter is very soft; consider blasting in the microwave for a few seconds. And do sift your flour. I know this sounds like extra admin, but it really helps make a beautiful, lightly textured sponge.

Preheat your oven to 160°C/350°F/gas 4, and double-line 3 round baking tins, sized at 10 cm/4 inches, 15 cm/6 inches and 20 cm/8 inches in diameter, with good-quality parchment paper. I use 3 shallow tins to bake the 3 layers of sponge needed per cake, but one taller tin will also do the trick. Double lining the tins is a pain, but it means that the outside of the sponge will colour less, making for a prettier edge of the cake.

In the largest bowl you can find, combine all your ingredients together in one go and mix well until you have a uniform batter with no lumps at all. This takes some welly, so you might want to use a food mixer or split the batter into two lots, if that's easier to manage. Don't forget to scrape down the sides to get all the sticky, sugary bits fully combined.

Taste a little at this point to ensure that you have your preferred intensity of lemon/lavender, and add more, if desired, remembering that the intensity of the lavender will increase as the cake bakes.

⊳⊳

Pour your mixture into each of your tins. Spread the mixture evenly, all the way to the edges, and make a slight well in the middle to ensure an even height of bake. The batter needs to be around 8 cm/3 inches deep in each tin.

Bake for around 40–45 minutes, until a skewer comes out clean and the sponge bounces back when pressed.

Meanwhile, prepare your buttercream by mixing the ingredients together well, until light and fluffy.

When baked, remove the cakes from their tins and allow to cool, then carefully trim each sponge into three equally sized layers (about 2½–3¾ cm/1–1¼ inches high) with a sharp knife. Try to cut the bottom piece of sponge and the top piece off, because they'll be the most coloured.

Fill your cakes by spreading a thin layer of buttercream between each layer, and gently stack them up, placing each cake on top of the correct-sized cake board.

Crumb-coat each cake (see page 46) and place in the fridge to chill for an hour.

For the final coat of icing, pluck some petals from your edible flowers and beat into the buttercream icing, then use a side scraper to apply a thin layer of icing all the way around, ensuring you have nice sharp edges. There's a top tip on this technique on page 46. Chill the cakes in the fridge once more.

Now you can tier up your cakes, using dowels to support the weight of each one. This internal support "scaffold" will balance the weight of the tiers and ensure they sit up nice and straight. Using supports also ensures that, if your cake has to sit on display in a warm room for a while before being served, it's less likely to collapse or slip. You can use food-safe wooden dowels, plastic ones, or jumbo straws (without the bendy bits!). I like to use wooden dowels for heavier/taller cakes, and strong drinking straws for lighter/smaller ones.

First, decide which side of your cake is the front. To do this, get down on a level with the cake and choose the angle that has the prettiest petals showing through and the straightest edges. Measure out the position that the next tier of cake will take on top of this tier, and draw an imaginary square within this space, inserting dowels at the four corners, ensuring that the dowels will definitely be tucked under the edge of the upper cake.

ᗡᗡ

Use a pencil to carefully mark out the place where the dowel needs to be cut, to make sure the top cake sits flush on the bottom tier. Remove the dowels from the cake and, using a sharp knife, trim off at the mark and re-insert into the cake. If your lower tier is at all wonky, now is your chance to correct this, by ensuring all of your dowels are cut to the same height as the tallest part of the cake tier. You can fill any visible gap under the upper cake with ribbon/more buttercream once it's in position – the most important thing is that it's level!

Spread a little royal icing on to the top of the lower cake and, carefully, using a palette knife, transfer the middle cake tier on to the base tier. If it's wonky when you've put it on, just gently push it into place with the tip of your palette knife resting on the base board.

Repeat until the cake is all tiered up.

Approximately 1–2 hours before serving, attach your flower petals. Edible flowers wilt very quickly, especially in warm summer weather, so apply just before you need to serve the cake.

If you're going for a full skirt effect (on your base tier), set aside your smallest and freshest blooms and gently press them into the buttercream, ensuring that no cake can be seen underneath.

For the scattered-petal effect (as on the middle tier), gently remove the petals you like best from the flowers, and gently press them into the buttercream.

For the gold leaf effect (on the top tier), gently press a single sheet of gold leaf directly onto the buttercream, and smooth on from the other side of the backing paper with a finger. Gently lift the paper off and re-position, if necessary, to achieve the coverage that you want.

WATERCOLOUR DRIP CAKE WITH PAPER FLOWERS

You will need

A tiered cake iced with
buttercream and raspberry
jam and covered in pale-pink
sugar-paste icing
(I made 2 batches of Victoria
sponge using the One-Bowl
Wonder recipe on page 20,
baked to make one 3-layer,
15-cm/6-inch round cake,
and one 3-layer, 10-cm/
4-inch round cake. These were
layered with buttercream
(see page 32) and raspberry
jam, then iced with sugar-paste
(recipe on page 37, technique
on page 46) and left to
set overnight.)

For the paint drips

2 tbsp cornflour
1 tbsp cold water, plus a few
more drips in order to get
the right consistency (thick,
but drippy)
Paste food colourings
(I used hot pink, bright yellow
and orange – you can mix
yellow and red for this last
one, if you prefer)

I love drip cakes! Why not do something a little different and jazz up your cake with some coloured drips? My tip is to practise your drips on the back of the cake first, so you get the hang of how much to use to get the desired length and thickness.

To tier your iced cake

Once your cake is layered, iced and chilled, you are ready to stack the smaller tier on top of the larger one. Before you do this, choose the "front" of each cake – most iced cakes have slight variations in the straightness of their edges and the flatness of their tops, so pick the prettiest part of your cakes for the front.

To support the upper tier, I use thick drinking straws (the kind you get with bubble tea) as supports, moving to wooden dowels for super-high or heavy cakes. Into the larger tier, insert 4 straws in a square shape, a maximum of 8 cm/ 3¼ inches apart. Push the straws down gently, in a vertical position (no wonky angles!) until they touch the base board. Then, using a sharp pair of scissors, snip off the tops of the straws, so that about 1–2 mm of straw is sticking out.

Apply a slick of royal icing over the top of the straws and, using a palette knife, carefully pick up the smaller tier and position it on top of the larger tier. Use the palm of your hand to gently position the top tier if it doesn't land perfectly.

For your edible watercolour paints

Into as many small bowls as you'd like colours, mix the cornflour, water and colouring together, until you have a nice thick, but still dripping, paste. Test this out on a piece of paper before dripping on to your cake.

To drizzle, dip a small food-safe paintbrush into the coloured mixture, and touch this against the top edge of the cake tier that you want to decorate. Start at the back and try a few different angles and techniques until you know how much to load up your brush to get the length of drip you're looking for. Repeat with the rest of your colours until you have the right number of drips – mixing the colours well each time, to prevent them separating. Allow the drips to dry before adding any other decorations. Dots of stiff peak royal icing secure these paper flowers to the cake (see overleaf for how to make them).

HANDMADE PAPER FLOWERS

You will need

Sharp scissors

Cocktail sticks or
    thick flower wire

Scrap paper or cotton wool

White craft glue

Florist or washi tapes in your
    fave colours

Faux stamens (available online,
    optional)

A pencil

Crêpe paper or thin, coloured
    craft paper of your choice for
    the petals

White craft glue

Royal icing (see page 34), for
    sticking the flowers to the cake

Paper flowers are such fun to make and they look so beautiful that I stockpile them to give as little gifts on friends' birthdays ... You can be truly creative, here, collecting scraps of paper from all sorts of places. Try to imagine the most ridiculous flower you can, and create it in paper! Paper flowers stick best to fondant-iced cakes.

Cut a cocktail stick in half and use the blunt end to create the central bud for your flower. To do this, scrunch up a small piece of scrap paper or cotton wool into a ball measuring around 1 cm/⅓ inch across. Create a small hole in the middle and, before inserting your cocktail stick, put a small dot of white glue in the hole. Insert the cocktail stick and hold for a few seconds until stuck.

Cut a 4-cm/1½-inch square of crêpe/craft paper and use this to cover the bud, wrapping it up completely, tucking the edges and corners of the paper under the bud and wrapping them around the stem. Secure in place with florist tape.

Take a group of around 6–8 stamens and fold in half so the little dots on the end all stick up at even heights. Tuck the middles of each stamen around the base of the bud, squeezing and shaping the wires to ensure that they stick up at regular-ish intervals around the bud. Secure by tightly wrapping florist tape around the base of each bud and a little way down the cocktail stick.

Using your crêpe paper or thin, coloured paper, draw a 5-petal shape as per the diagram in the picture opposite left, then carefully cut it out.

Gently shape each of the petals a little with your fingertips, stretching and softening the paper to form rounded, slightly concave petal shapes. Crimp the base of the petal shape, folding it to create a crinkled effect – this helps to attach it to the stem.

Carefully wrap the base of the first of the petals around the stem and, using the folds you've already made, push and wrap each of the petals around the bud and wire, holding in place with one hand and feeding the folded paper in with the other. Gently pull the petals upwards and outwards as you go, to ensure they're evenly spread, and attach to the stem with florist tape, continuing to wrap this at least halfway down the cocktail stick to secure.

BAKING AND ICING NAKED AND SEMI-NAKED CAKES

There are lots of definitions of naked and semi-naked cakes, but I think of it like this: naked cakes have icing between layers, but their edges are left un-iced, and therefore look quite "rustic" and casual; semi-naked cakes again have icing between layers, but their edges are also iced with a crumb-coat, so, seen from the side, they have lovely straight edges, with just a bit of cake crumb showing through.

Some people think that making beautiful naked cakes is easier than making fully iced ones, but I think there is still a lot of skill involved. Each cake layer should be exactly the same thickness, crisp at the edges, with no pieces missing, and the icing should always be applied in a pretty way, to make the cake look properly "finished" and not just flung together.

GENERAL TIPS FOR BAKING NAKED CAKES

- If baking a lighter-coloured sponge, e.g. Victoria sponge or madeira, double line your baking tin with parchment and bake 5°C/40°F lower than normal, to ensure the edges don't become discoloured.

- Make sure that the batter is pushed right to the edges of the cake tins before baking, with a well in the middle, so that your sponge has a nice flat top. If the sponge still peaks in the middle after baking, level it off with a knife before layering up and icing.

- Consider weighing your cake batter to get exactly the same amount of cake per tin.

- Bake each layer separately, e.g. 3 tins at 15 cm/6 inches round, to ensure the edges don't get too dark during baking.

- Trim each layer to exactly the same height (use a ruler!) so the cake looks beautifully even.

- Pick the prettiest sections of the sponge and put these at the front! Carefully cut, grate or trim off any ugly bits, or hide them with some icing or a piece of fruit! It's simple but effective – we always choose the straightest, smartest-looking part of the cake for the front at Bee's Bakery.

GENERAL TIPS FOR ICING NAKED CAKES

- Use iced cake-boards trimmed with ribbon under each cake, and ensure that you have an internal scaffold in place to support the weight of each tier. See page 76 for instructions.

- Allow each layer to fully chill before stacking them up, to make sure they don't "squidge".

- When decorating a naked cake, use proper butter buttercream, rather than Swiss meringue buttercream.

- Cream-cheese icing is not strong enough to support the weight of tiered cakes, and slips terribly in warmer months. My advice: don't use it unless it's winter or you can guarantee the cake can be fully chilled before serving.

- Consider using coloured icings on different tiers to add interest – pastels and pale or tonal colours work best; too many colours, or really intense ones, can look OTT.

- Consider using fancy piping nozzles to create different effects.

- Fully chill naked cakes before display, and make sure they're not out in the warm for more than 1–2 hours before serving, as naked cakes are more prone to slipping and squashing in warm weather.

PIPED NAKED WEDDING CAKE WITH EDIBLE FLOWERS

The "naked" wedding-cake style has become very popular in the past 3 years, and our signature style often involves the edible roses and other blooms that we've used in this recipe.

The edible flowers we use at the bakery are grown lovingly and with great skill by Jan Billington, in Devon. Jan is a certified organic grower and Soil Association hero and has the most beautiful flower fields I've ever seen. She is a great supplier, with sustainable farming methods (and her little Jack Russell terrier, Lily, keeps moles, voles and other flower-eating animals at bay by being the perfect guard dog!).

You will need

3 tiers of 3-layer sponge (I used a chocolate beetroot sponge at 20 cm/8 inches, a pistachio sponge at 15 cm/6 inches, and a dinky little rose cake at 10 cm/ 4 inches diameter)

Cake boards in corresponding sizes, trimmed with ribbon

Dowels/chunky straws to support the weight of each tier

Enough buttercream of your choosing to fill and cover (if needed) your cake (I used 3 x batches of vanilla buttercream, page 32)

Two piping bags, a large, round-tipped nozzle and a number 4 nozzle

Edible flowers, in your choice of colour and size

Bake your cake layers and allow to cool before layering them up and tiering according to the instructions on pages 74–76. For this cake, fill the top two tiers with a regular layer of buttercream, and cover the very top tier with a basic crumb coat. For the bottom tier, use a large, round-tipped piping nozzle with the buttercream to create a frilly-edge effect.

▷▷

To do this, pipe large, regular-shaped dots of icing in a circle around the edge of your tier, then make a smaller circle of dots inside this, and repeat, filling in the gaps as you get towards the middle. Chill the cake layer without the top layer added before assembly to make sure that the icing doesn't all squish out of the sides! Repeat for the next layer.

To achieve the piped effect around the sides of the cake, I traced out a little rough design on paper, and started piping carefully, using the index finger of my non-dominant hand to help guide the nozzle as I copied the design. My top tip here is to start at the back of the cake! My first few attempts are normally a little bit ropey, so I warm up on the parts of the cake that won't be seen most of the time, and, by the time I get round to the front, I'm well into the swing of it!

Chill the entire cake, to make sure the piped design looks super sharp and crisp. Finally, add the edible flowers by gently placing them on the top or sides of each tier, securing them with a dot of buttercream, where needed.

LAYERED VEGAN CHEESECAKE

**MAKES ONE 3-LAYER, 15-CM/
6-INCH ROUND CHEESECAKE**

For the base
60 g/2 oz/½ cup pumpkin seeds
60 g/2 oz/½ cup sunflower seeds
60 g/2 oz/⅓ cup buckwheat
  groats or puffed quinoa
  or pine nuts
20 g/¾ oz/⅛ cup cacao nibs
  or 2 tsp cocoa powder
120 g/4¼ oz/⅔ cup soft pitted
  dates (e.g. medjool), chopped
3 tbsp coconut oil, melted
2 tsp vanilla-bean extract
1–3 tbsp water (if needed)

Cheesecake layers
300 g/10½ oz/2½ cups cashew
  nuts, soaked in cold water for
  at least 2 hours, or overnight
100 g/3½ oz/⅔ cup almonds
  or hazelnuts, soaked in cold
  water for at least 2 hours,
  or overnight
130 ml/4½ fl oz/½ cup almond
  milk
80 g/2¾ oz/¼ cup raw honey or
  maple syrup
100 g/3½ oz/½ cup coconut oil,
  melted
6 tsp lemon juice
3 tsp blueberry powder
3 tsp raspberry fruit powder

To serve
Fresh raspberries, blueberries
  and edible flowers

I first came across the idea of a nut-based "cheesecake" when watching vegan videos made by Laura Miller, my most favourite YouTube presenter. To be honest, the idea had never occurred to me before, and I was really intrigued by it.

Cashew nuts form the base of this recipe, but there are lots of other amazing, interesting ingredients that help to build this beautiful cake. The colours come from fruit powders, so no E-numbers here! It's not the cheapest recipe on the planet, so I cut it into pieces and freeze it, and it lasts ages. Don't forget to pre-soak the nuts, as this activates them and makes them easier to blend.

For the base
Line a 15-cm/6-inch round cake tin with strong cling film.

Pulse all of the base ingredients together in a food processor a few times to get started, then continue to blend for about a minute, until the mix starts sticking together.

Tip the mixture into the cake tin and press down with the back of a spoon or your hands, until it's nice and smooth and even. Freeze until ready to use.

For the cheesecake layers
Drain and rinse the cashews and almonds, then blend only these two together in the food mixer until completely smooth – pulse on high and low alternately to ensure all the big pieces are broken down.

Add the remaining ingredients, except the fruit powders, and blend until smooth.

Now divide the mix into 3 bowls, and add the fruit powders (I made one mixture with blueberry powder, one mixture with raspberry powder and left the third plain), and mix until you have a beautiful bright, fruity colour.

Remove the base layer from the freezer and pour one of your coloured mixtures on top first, ensuring it's even. Return to the freezer for 2 hours, then pour on the next coloured layer and repeat. If you prefer, you could do thinner layers of each for a stripy effect.

Decorate with fresh fruit and edible flowers, and serve.

BEST CHERRY BEER ICE-CREAM CAKE

MAKES A 15-CM/6-INCH ROUND CAKE

For the cake layers
260 ml/9 fl oz/1 cup Kriek (cherry beer) or other dark beer (e.g. stout, porter or raspberry beer)
250 g/8¾ oz/1⅛ cup butter
375 g/13¼ oz/1⅔ cups light soft brown sugar
80 g/2¾ oz/⅔ cup cocoa powder
2 eggs
150 ml/5¼ fl oz/⅔ cup soured cream, crème fraîche or plain yogurt
1 tsp vanilla-bean extract
300 g/10½ oz/2⅓ cups self-raising flour

For the ice-cream layers
6 egg yolks
165 g/5¾ oz/¾ cup light soft brown sugar
568 ml/20 fl oz/2⅓ cups double cream
225 ml/8 fl oz/1 cup coffee porter or any other beer you fancy (not a hoppy one, though!)

To decorate
Cherries dipped in melted chocolate (dark, milk or white)
1 x batch of Swiss meringue buttercream icing (page 36)

My buddies, Jonny and Brad, run the Craft Beer Channel on YouTube and we have filmed a few fun baking videos together recently – have a little google! These boys are always up for trying jazzy new beery baking ideas, which is why and how we came up with this beautiful beer ice-cream recipe. I've combined it with another fantastic beer-licious recipe I wrote for them – a beautiful, dark, moist cherry beer cake – and when you combine the two, it's heaven in a bite! You will need an ice-cream maker for this recipe.

For the cake layers
Preheat your oven to 160°C/350°F/gas 4 and line three shallow, or one deep, 15-cm/6-inch round baking tins with tinfoil.

Pour the beer into a medium-sized saucepan, then add the butter and sugar, and heat them all together gently over a medium heat until the butter is just melted. Don't boil the mixture or the beautiful beery flavour will be lost. Add in the cocoa powder whilst the mix is still warm, to make a ridiculously beery, buttery thick goo – this is the base for your cake.

Allow to cool for a couple of minutes whilst you stir your eggs, soured cream and vanilla together in a separate bowl, until you have a creamy paste. Pour the creamy, eggy mixture into the now-cool beery base and mix well.

Sift your flour to make sure there are no lumpy bits, and add to the mix.

Pour your batter into your lined tins to get three equal-height layers, or one deep layer, and bake for around 25 minutes (for 3 layers) or 45 minutes (for one deep layer), until the sponge bounces back a little when pressed.

Allow the sponge to cool before cutting into 3 layers (only necessary if you've baked the one deep cake).

▷▷

For the ice-cream layers
Line a deep 15-cm/6-inch round baking tin with strong cling film.

Mix your egg yolks and sugar together in a saucepan, then add the double cream. Stirring slowly, bring the mixture to a light simmer over a gentle heat. Do not let this boil or stick to the sides.

When the mixture just reaches simmer point, pour in the beer, give it a good stir to get some of the bubbles out, then remove from the heat. Allow to cool, then cover with cling film and leave to rest overnight in the fridge. It really needs to be super chilled before you do the next step.

If your ice-cream maker is the type that has a bowl that needs to be pre-frozen, do this overnight too.

At least 3 hours before you want to serve your cake, set your ice-cream maker on "churn" and slowly pour half of the super-chilled mix into the churner. Meanwhile, place one of the sponge layers in the cling-film-lined cake tin to form the base of the ice-cream cake.

Once the ice cream has come to the "soft serve" stage, normally at around 15–20 minutes, scoop it out and freeze for at least 30 minutes. Whilst this is freezing, churn the next half of your ice cream.

Once the ice cream in the freezer is cold enough to hold its shape, spread a good layer on top of the cake layer and refreeze. By this time, your next batch of ice cream will be ready to move from the ice-cream maker to the freezer.

Continue layering up with more cake, then more ice cream, until you run out of both! Return the whole cake to the freezer for at least 2 hours before serving.

To decorate
Once the cake is frozen, and you are ready to serve, decorate with the Swiss meringue buttercream and whip up some peaks to resemble the frothy head on a good beer. Then top with the chocolate-dipped cherries, before serving.

BEE'S BAKERY CHRISTMAS CAKE

MAKES A 20-CM/8-INCH ROUND CAKE

To soak, the day before baking

900 g/2 lb/5⅓ cups dried fruits of your choice (e.g. apricots, dates, figs, prunes, glacé cherries, dried blueberries, and candied peel), chopped into regularly sized, smallish pieces

500 g/1lb 1⅔ oz/3 cups dried vine fruits of your choice (e.g. blackcurrants, raisins, sultanas (golden raisins) – those giant California flame raisins are great – or cranberries)

8–10 tbsp liquid (e.g. a mixture of orange and cranberry juice, cool black Earl Grey tea, brandy or another spirit)

Zest and juice of 1 large orange and 1 big lemon (NB: this juice counts towards the 8–10 tbsp of liquid, listed above)

For the cake batter

350 g/12⅓ oz/1½ cups butter, soft (at room temperature)

300 g/10½ oz/1⅓ cups soft brown sugar (a combination of light brown and darker muscovado works well – use more of the former for a light sponge, and more of the latter if you want a bit more colour)   **>>**

I LOVE a Christmas fruitcake, which makes me a bit old-fashioned, right? Wrong, Scrooges! Let me be clear, though: I'm talking *my* Christmas cake – a lighter, tastier, more-sponge, less-fruit Christmas cake. One that has beautiful plump pieces of easily identifiable, high-quality dried fruits, and is not jam-packed full of miscellaneous clumps of bitter-tasting, black-coloured maybe-raisins and something-like-sultanas that stick to your fillings and make your jaw ache. Mine's not quite as intense as that – in fact, mine could be called "fruitcake for wimps" . . .

I'm not going to be shy about this one – this recipe is utter genius and every fruitcake hater I've ever tried it out on (sometimes forcibly) eventually concedes that it's pretty good.

I tend to bake my Christmas cake in late November/early December, before things go completely mad at the bakery with Christmas orders. If you're likely to have a hectic run-up to Christmas, too, you can do the same – just store your fruitcake, wrapped in parchment and then foil, in a super-clean tin and it'll keep for around 6 weeks.

Tips for a beautiful Christmas cake

○ This recipe is really forgiving, so choose fruits that you and your family and friends really love, as the final cake will still be a cracker.

○ Go heavy on the apricots and cherries if you want a lighter, fresher-tasting cake. Go heavy on the figs and prunes if you fancy a rich, dark-coloured cake.

○ Soak your fruits overnight before making the cake – it makes all the difference.

○ Don't feel you need to feed your cake with alcohol – by presoaking the fruit in juice or tea, and choosing lighter, more flavoursome fruits, there's no real need to add in the booze, in my opinion – just keep the cake well wrapped.

ᗡᗡ

5 large free-range eggs

100 g/3½ oz/1 cup ground almonds

350 g/12⅓ oz/2¾ cups plain (all-purpose) flour (a mixture of white and wholemeal is great)

1 tsp baking powder

150 g/5¼ oz/1¼ cups shelled and roughly chopped nuts (I especially love pecans, but hazelnuts or almonds are good too, and less expensive)

To serve (optional)

1 kg/2 lb 3¼ oz marzipan

Icing (powdered) sugar

The day before you want to bake the cake, prepare your fruit by warming your liquid in a small pan, or popping in the microwave for 20 seconds (do not boil it), and pour it over all of your dried fruit and zest in a bowl. Mix thoroughly and leave to cool and soak overnight. Your fruit will be juicy and plump in the morning – perfect for baking. Leave your butter out of the fridge overnight too, to soften up.

The next day, before starting to prepare your cake batter, preheat your oven to 160°C/350°F/gas 4 and double line a 20- or 23-cm/8- or 9-inch round baking tin with parchment, leaving about 2 cm/1 inch sticking out of the top of the tin. If you only have an 18-cm/7-inch tin, then just bake the remaining mix in a couple of muffin cases – baker's perks!

Combine the butter with the sugars in a food mixer (or use a hand-held mixer), or if you're working on toning up your biceps, go for it by mixing by hand in a large bowl. Cream until a light, fluffy mixture is formed – the fluffier, the better.

Add in the eggs, a couple at a time, with a little spoonful of the almonds in between, to stop the mixture curdling. Once combined, add in the flour, baking powder and the remainder of the ground almonds, plus the nuts, and mix briefly. Then add in the presoaked fruit – there shouldn't be much liquid at the bottom of the bowl, but do add in any dribbles that are left. Mix well, scraping down the sides of the bowl to make sure everything is combined.

Pour the mixture into your cake tin – it should be around ¾ full – and ensure the top of the mix is flat, so you get a nice evenly topped cake. Place two circles of parchment on top of the cake – this stops it getting too dark in the oven.

Bake for 1 hour at 160°C/350°F/gas 4, then turn the cake around (in case your oven has any hot spots), reduce the temperature to 150°C/325°F/gas 3, and bake for around 1–1.5 hours more.

After the second hour, check the cake to see whether it's done – insert a skewer or the tip of a thin-bladed knife into the middle; when it's done, there might be a couple of crumbs sticking to the knife, but there should be no raw mixture.

Leave the cake to cool inside the tin, so that it keeps its shape, and, when cool, either dust a little bit of icing sugar on the top to serve, or cover in marzipan and decorate however you like! I used a marzipan icing on my cake (covering the sponge with a nice thick layer, using the same technique as I do for sugar-paste icing, see page 46), and arranged some Christmas decorations and a little log cabin on top – with lots of icing sugar sprinkled over for a snowy effect.

MACDUFF MODERN TARTAN CAKE

**MAKES A 4-LAYER, 20-CM/
8-INCH ROUND CAKE**

You will need
2 batches of One-Bowl Wonder
   sponge cake mixture
   (see page 20)
Paste food colours (I used
   orange, red extra, royal blue
   and mint green for the cake
   and yellow for the buttercream)
1 batch of buttercream icing for
   filling the cakes (see page 32),
   coloured yellow with the paste
   food colouring
2 batches of chocolate
   buttercream (see page 35)

A ruler and pencil
Some cardboard (e.g. an empty
   cereal box)
Sharp, fine-pointed knife
Sharp scissors

I was born in and spent the first few years of my life in a small town called Macduff, on the part of the north-east Scottish coast that Shakespeare wrote a play about. I remember the freezing weather, the local dialect we spoke, and feeding the seals my after-school chips off the harbour wall!

Our family tartan is technically Nisbett or McNab, but the MacDuff clan tartan is more colourful, so I designed this cake around the colourways in that design. This one's for you, MacDuff!

For the cake
Preheat your oven to 180°C/400°F/gas 6 and line 4 round 20-cm/8-inch cake tins with good-quality parchment.

Weigh out equal amounts of the cake batter into 4 bowls, adding your choice of gel or paste food colouring to each bowl.

Pour into separate tins – one for each colour – and bake for around 20–25 minutes, until a cocktail stick inserted into the sponge comes out clean.

Allow to cool whilst you prepare your buttercream.

To assemble
Start by checking that the heights of all 4 sponge layers are equal, at about 3.2 cm/1¼ inches tall, trimming any excess off if needed.

Following the diagram on page 103, draw 3 concentric circles, onto a piece of sturdy card as follows: outer circle: 20 cm/8 inch diameter; middle circle: 13½ cm/5½ inch diameter; centre circle, 7 cm/3 inch diameter. Cut them out.

▷▷

Placing the card circles on top of your cakes as a guide, carefully trim your cooled cake layers using the tip of a super-sharp, fine-pointed knife held vertically, so you have three different-sized cake rings per layer of cake.

Using a small palette or butter knife, carefully spread a thin line of yellow buttercream around the inside edge of each of your circles and gently press the circles together, as shown. Arrange your differently coloured cake rings in a way that means that no ring is next to another ring of the same colour, both horizontally and vertically when you stack the layers up. Follow the chart below as a handy guide as to how the layers should stack up.

Build your cake up by spreading a thicker layer of yellow buttercream between each layer, then allow to chill in the fridge before crumb coating (see page 46).

Chill again, then decorate using the chocolate buttercream – I used a rough country-style finish.

Chill until serving – this helps the cake to keep its awesome sharp layers.

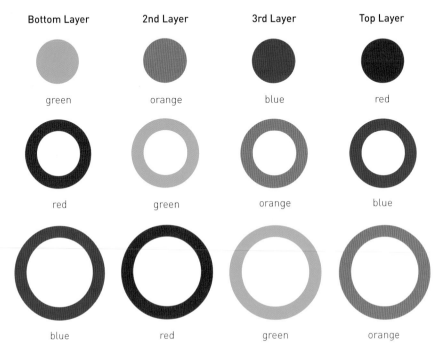

Bottom Layer	2nd Layer	3rd Layer	Top Layer
green	orange	blue	red
red	green	orange	blue
blue	red	green	orange

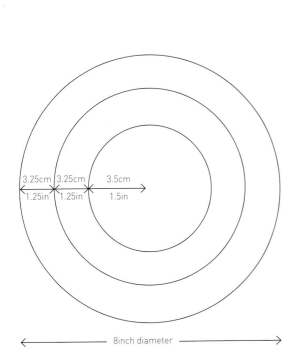

3.25cm
1.25in

3.25cm
1.25in

3.5cm
1.5in

8inch diameter

EDIBLE GLASS SHARD CAKE

For the cake

A layered, filled and iced cake of
your choosing

For the edible glass

750 g/1 lb 10½ oz/3¾ cups
white caster (superfine) or
granulated sugar

450 g/1 lb/1⅓ cups light corn
syrup or glucose syrup

240 ml/8 fl oz/1 cup water

To finish

A small amount of gel paste food
colouring, e.g. Sugarflair paste
in egg yellow

Sprinkles, as required (avoid
using chocolate ones, as
they'll melt!)

Gold/silver balls (optional)

Edible glitter (optional)

Gold lustre dust (optional)

Edible gold leaf (optional)

Crystallized flower petals
(optional)

Making edible glass, or sugar shards, at home is fiddly and you need a sugar thermometer, but it creates a brilliant effect for decorating cakes. The basic sugar recipe is easy to customize and adapt, so you can really personalize it to suit the cake. Adding in gel paste colours works well, as does adding sprinkles, silver or gold balls, edible glitter, lustre powder or even crystallized flower petals – so get creative.

Prepare a large baking sheet and line with a silicon mat, or a well-greased sheet of parchment. Prepare a large bowl of iced water (large enough to fit your saucepan into) and set aside.

In a heavy-bottomed saucepan, pour the sugar, syrup and water, and stir to combine. Continue to stir over a medium heat until the sugar begins to dissolve. If sugar crystals attach to the side of the pan, scrape them into the main mix.

Put your sugar thermometer into the pan, ensuring the base is covered by the mix, and, *without stirring*, bring the mixture to the boil until it reaches 150°C/ 300°F. Be really careful at this stage; don't move the pan as it's boiling, and carefully remove from the heat when it reaches the correct temperature. You can test whether the sugar mix is ready to pour by carefully spooning a tiny amount into a clear bowl or heatproof glass of cold water – when a droplet of the mix is added to the water, it should form a thin thread that breaks easily when it's cool.

As soon as you've removed the pan from the heat, dunk it into the bowl of iced water for a few seconds, being careful not to get any of the water inside the pan. This stops the sugar cooking and keeps it at the right consistency.

At this point, you can pour half your mixture into another pan and colour the two hot sugar mixes by adding your choice of colours and sprinkles, as you like. Work quickly, as the sugar will start to set. Once done, pour a thin layer of the molten sugar on to your parchment paper, using a spatula or metal spoon to move it around, if needed (see picture overleaf).

Allow to cool and harden, then use the back of a metal spoon (or a hammer) to break the sugar into shards. These can be kept in a Tupperware contained for up to a month. To attach to the cake, you may need a tiny dot of leftover syrup, or some piping gel, to stick each shard in place.

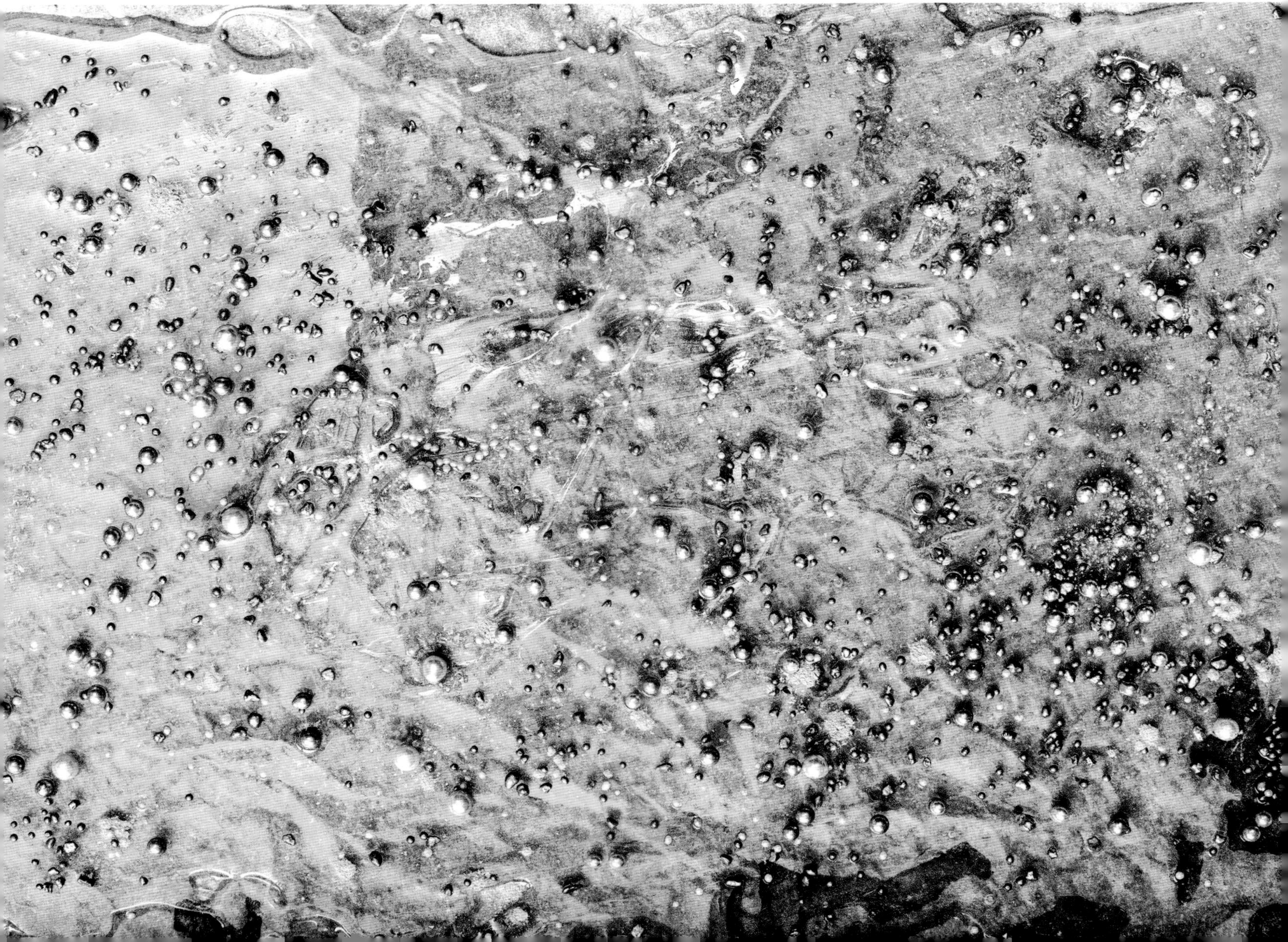

AMAZING JOCONDE CAKE

For the inside cake

1 x 3-layer baked sponge cake
   to a recipe of your choosing
1 x batch of buttercream of
   your choosing
Jam (optional)

For the design, you will need

Graph paper
Scissors
Ruler
Pencil
Good-quality food safe
   waxed paper or
   strong parchment paper
A thin-nibbed pen that can draw
   on plastic, e.g. Sharpie

For baking, you will need

Stand mixer
Several small bowls
Large silicon mat
Large baking tray
Piping bags
Spatulas – small and large

>>

I first came across this style of cake in the USA, where an incredible cake designer called M. Robin has been leading the pack for years. It's technically an old-skool French patisserie technique, but the elements of graphic design involved in this one bring it right up to date. The technique involves making several coloured cake pastes and piping a design you like on to parchment, before pouring a layer of sponge batter on top and baking. This fuses the two layers together and creates a pattern within the sponge. Once the sponge panel is baked, it is then wrapped around a central cake, like a sheet of icing, to decorate.

This cake offers the opportunity to get really creative – but it is a true project, and you'll need to be super-organized to pull it off.

This recipe makes enough to decorate a 13-cm/5-inch, 3-layer cake, already iced (make sure you have this ready before you begin).

First, measure the circumference and height of your baking tin, then cut out a rectangle of graph paper to these dimensions.

Next, get creative to make your own joconde cake design! I love triangle and hexagon shapes on cakes, and often take inspiration from wrapping paper or greetings cards that I've received. There are also lots of ready-designed stencil templates available online, e.g. on Pinterest, so use one of these if you need a bit of help.

Draw out the design on your paper rectangle, remembering to leave a good-sized border around any shapes, so that there's room to trim off any browned edges, if necessary. Sometimes, I like to colour in the paper stencil so I can remember which colours I want when I'm ready to bake.

For the paste you'll use to create the patterns

60 g/2 oz/¼ cup butter, softened but not melted
1 egg white
1 tsp vanilla-bean extract
45 g/1⅔ oz/⅓ cup icing (powdered) sugar
45 g/1⅔ oz/⅓ cup plain (all-purpose) flour
Paste food colours of your choice (I used turquoise, yellow, grey and green)
1½ tsp poppy or chia seeds (optional, but adds a cool speckle)

For the sponge batter

2 egg whites
2½ tsp caster (superfine) sugar
3 eggs
85 g/3 oz/1 cup ground almonds
75 g/2⅔ oz/ ⅔ cup icing (powdered) sugar
25 g/1 oz/¼ cup plain (all-purpose) flour
30 g/1 oz/¼ cup butter, melted
White paste food colouring (optional)

For the stencil-pattern paste

Cream your butter, egg white, vanilla and icing sugar together in a food mixer until light and fluffy and paler in colour – scrape down the sides of the bowl to ensure all is incorporated.

Add in the flour and mix again, then divide up the batter into small bowls according to the number of colours that you need and how much of each, and add in your food colouring and poppy/chia seeds (if using), mixing well. If you're using the seeds, only add them to colours where you'd like a speckled effect, and remember that they will show up better in paler colours. Some colours will deepen over time, especially the reds, blues and greens, so bear this in mind too. Fill a separate piping bag for each colour.

Place your silicon mat on to your baking tray, then your pattern stencil, and then a layer of oiled parchment. You need to be able to see your stencil through the parchment. Pipe your design directly onto the parchment, tracing over your stencil. Make sure that your edges are nice and sharp, and that there is an even coverage (e.g. no holes) of batter.

There should be enough batter to repeat the pattern twice. Two layers are handy in case one breaks during the final assembly.

When the design is complete, refrigerate for 20 minutes whilst you preheat your oven and make the batter for the joconde sponge.

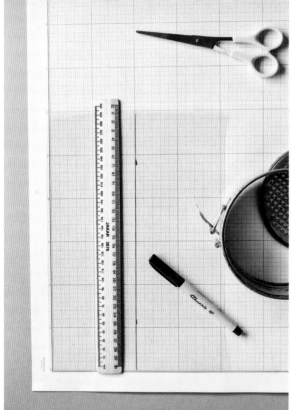

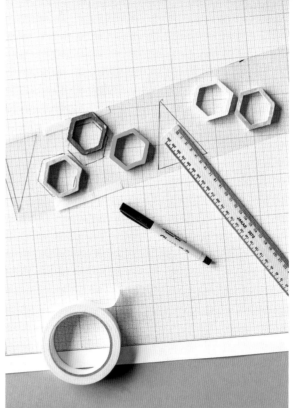

For the main joconde sponge
Preheat your oven to 200°C/425°F/gas 7.

Using a stand mixer, whisk up your egg whites until they're a little light and frothy, then very slowly add in the caster sugar, a little at a time, continuing to whisk, until you reach the stiff, shiny peak stage – this may take a few minutes.

Pour the egg-white mixture into a separate bowl, then, in the stand mixer bowl, mix the whole eggs with the ground almonds, icing sugar and plain flour, gradually adding the ingredients until you have a light smooth mixture.

Very gently, fold around one-third of the egg-white mixture into this new mixture, then add the remainder slowly, keeping as much air in the batter as you can – mix as little as possible.

Finally, fold in the melted butter and mix for a few seconds only, until it's combined.

Remove the chilled stencil patterns from the fridge and gently pour the batter over the top, using a palette knife to smooth it out evenly, whilst being careful not to dig into the pattern below. It will form a thin layer on top.

Bake in the upper part of the hot oven for 4–6 minutes, until the sponge is just beginning to colour and bounces back when pressed – do not let it turn too brown. Remove from the oven and allow to cool. Cover tightly with cling film, if not using straight away.

Remeasure the dimensions your sponge will need to be to ensure it fits all the way around your cake, then trim the cake strips to match, chopping off any browned edges/excess length. It's useful to have two, in case one cracks or the colours have spread.

To assemble your cake
Pop your pre-iced cake on to a plate or cake stand and take one of the cake strips, laying the bottom edge against the bottom of the cake, parchment side out, pressing it gently on to the cake, all the way around. Gently and carefully, peel back and remove the parchment from the cake to reveal your pattern.

Trim the end a little if necessary, and secure the join with some buttercream. Even out the top of the cake by spreading with more buttercream, and chill for 20 minutes before enjoying.

PRINTED ICING SHOWSTOPPER WITH ORGANIC BLOOMS

You will need

A baked, layered and sugar-paste/fondant iced cake in any recipe and icing of your choosing (I used a 4-tier cake, at 25-, 20-, 15- and 10-cm/ 10-, 8-, 6- and 4-inch rounds, with 3 layers per tier)

Pre-printed edible icing sheets, allowed to dry for at least 30 minutes

Piping gel

A pastry brush

A cake smoother

Organic flowers, to decorate (see notes overleaf)

Royal icing, to attach flowers (optional)

Edible gold leaf sheets (optional)

I first heard about printed cakes from this amazing edible artist called Stevi Auble, based in Palm Springs, who prints amazing bespoke designs on to wafer paper. Stevi is a qualified graphic designer and I am a qualified microbiologist with few discernible artistic skills; however, I'm not going to let the fact that I cannot draw a beautiful flower from scratch stop me from creating a really gorgeous botanical illustrated cake design. There are some lovely downloadable designs and templates available online these days (try Pinterest and Shutterstock as a start), so you don't have to be a total artist to create something beautiful.

You can also get hold of sheets of edible printable paper from lots of online shops; often, they will print any high-resolution image you like, or design something specific for you. The paper we use at the bakery is called Decorice Professional and is available online. We use a Canon edible printer with edible ink. As a general rule, one A4 sheet of icing will be enough to ice one 15-cm/ 6-inch round cake of no more than 9 cm/3.5 inches in height.

To attach the printed icing to your cake

Measure, mark and trim your icing sheets first of all, to ensure they'll fit around your cake. You will need more than one sheet to go around the larger tiers.

Flip the printed icing sheet on its front and gently peel back the plastic protector sheet. Apply a liberal coat of piping gel using a pastry brush, making sure you have even coverage all the way to the edges.

Gently lift the printed icing sheet and rest the bottom edge against the base of the cake, making sure it's straight at the bottom of the cake. Smooth the icing sheet over the sugar-paste icing using your hands, ensuring there are no bubbles or wrinkles.

Before attaching the second sheet, check it's the right size and trim off any excess, as an overlap will show up and often peel away from the cake.

⟩⟩

Repeat the process and, once all sheets are attached, give the surface a gentle smooth with a cake smoother, to ensure any edges are fully stuck down.

To attach the real blooms
First of all, you need to be careful that you're not using poisonous flowers. It's best to double check with your florist, or use a certified organic florist such as Maddocks Farm (see Stockists on page 144).

Secondly, it's best if the stems of the flowers you're using (unless they are edible petals) do not touch the cake, as you never know what bucket of dirty water they've been hanging out in before you got your hands on them. To avoid this, you can purchase little plastic flower plugs to put the ends of the flowers into. An even simpler solution is to apply a thin layer of cling film or white parchment to the area of cake that you know is going to be covered with flowers and attach it to the cake with royal icing. This creates a barrier that you can then stick the flowers straight on to.

If your blooms are super heavy, consider using a brand new hairpin or a few cocktail sticks to support the weight of them.

Bear in mind that your blooms will wilt after a couple of hours of being without water, so decorate with them just before you need them.

Using edible gold leaf
On this cake, I used a pretty edible gold leaf on one of the tiers – it's an expensive technique but it does look super glitzy! To apply the gold leaf to the sugar-paste icing, dampen the area you want to cover with water or piping gel, then gently press a sheet of gold leaf on to the area, slowly peeling the backing paper off. A dry paintbrush can help ease the gold leaf on to the cake, if necessary. You can repeat this to achieve fuller coverage, but I quite like a rough-edged effect too.

MIDNIGHT-BLUE PARTY CAKE WITH NEON PIPING AND SUGAR FLOWERS

You will need

A crumb-coated and chilled
cake of your choosing (I used
a 5-tiered cake, with tiers
measuring 30-, 25-, 20-, 15-
and 10-cm/12-, 10-, 8-, 6- and
4-inches round, with
3 layers of sponge per tier)

Sugar-paste/ready-to-roll
fondant icing (as a guide,
1 kg is usually enough to cover
a 20-cm/8-inch round cake, so
multiply accordingly)

Paste food colouring in navy blue,
midnight blue or royal blue,
and charcoal colours – you'll
use more than you think

Brand new rubber or plastic
gloves (optional, but a very
good idea!)

An apron

A thin-tipped knife
or cocktail stick

Cornflour

A rolling pin

Cake smoothers

A scribe tool or a clean pin
(optional)

Cake boards measuring 35-,
30-, 25-, 20-, 15- and 10-cm/
14-, 12-, 10-, 8-, 6- and
4-inches round   >>

I'm not a huge advocate for using large amounts of food colours. However, this cake is so striking – the dark colour really makes the piping details pop – that, for a special occasion, I think it's totally justified. Maybe just don't think about it too hard for once!

Hand-piping patterns has been falling out of fashion lately, but, secretly, I love doing it – so I updated a classic design using bold colours, and I love the way it looks.

You do need patience, a steady hand (and a great playlist) to master this cake, so it's worth setting some time aside to enjoy the process.

To colour your icing

First, colour your fondant icing by flattening the icing on the worktop, then spreading a copious amount of paste colouring all over its surface, before kneading the colour evenly into the icing. It's a good idea to wear a pair of box-fresh rubber or plastic gloves for this job to avoid getting stained hands, and an apron to avoid getting the pigment on your clothes. Repeat the process until the icing is just one or two shades lighter than you're looking for, as often the colour will darken over time.

If you have time, wrap the icing in cling film and leave for around an hour to deepen in colour. If the icing starts to crack, or looks like it's getting dry, add a splash of fresh cold water to it – this will improve elasticity and make it easier to use.

To ice your cake

When you're ready, put your crumb-coated cake on the worktop, in a position that has a bit of clear space around it. Remove any rings, bracelets, watches etc., as these can mark and scuff the icing.

Ribbon to attach around the base of each tier of cake (optional)
Piping bags
Royal icing at stiff peak consistency (see page 34), coloured using neon paste food colourings
Sugar paste/flower paste, coloured using neon paste food colourings
A hard rolling mat or clean hard worksurface, smeared with a little white vegetable fat or coconut oil

Roll the icing out on to a cornflour-dusted work surface, until around 2 cm/¾ inch thick. Use only the bare minimum of cornflour to avoid sticking, and be super careful not to get any on top of the icing, as it'll mark it with white scuffs. My top tip to make this easier is to turn the icing regularly, and to roll in lots of different directions (e.g. left to right, top to bottom, diagonally), as you'll be stronger in one direction than you think.

Roll the icing back on to the rolling pin, until you have just about 10 cm/4 inches hanging off the end, with all the rest tucked around the rolling pin. Drape the end over the closest edge of the cake to you, ensuring there is just enough spare on the work surface (I mean about 2 cm/¾ inch, but no more).

Gently and quickly roll the rolling pin away from you, covering the top of the cake with your icing, and draping it down the far side of the cake. The weak spots are the edges of the cake, and the icing can tear here quite easily, so quickly lose the rolling pin and use the palms of your hands to ensure the sides of the cake are covered and the icing is smoothly sticking to the entire cake. Avoid pressing with your fingertips, as you'll get little marks and your fingerprints will show up (see technique on page 46).

Use your cake smoothers like paddles, and gently rub them all over the cake, smoothing out any finger marks, little lumps or bumps, and making sure that your sides are nice and straight. If there are any air bubbles in the icing, use a scribe tool/ clean pin to pop them – try angling the pin upwards, at about a 45-degree angle, so the mark can't be seen from the top of the cake.

To achieve a really sharp edge on your cake, use one paddle vertically and one horizontally to encourage the two areas of fondant together. Start gently until you get the knack of it, then you can see how vigorous you can get away with being.

Layer your tiers, as per the instructions on pages 74–76. The bottom tier can sit on a cake board simply covered with sugar paste and trimmed with ribbon for a really professional finish.

Allow the cake to rest for an hour or, better still, overnight before piping – this'll firm up the icing and make it easier to pipe on to.

Pipe your details on to the cake, following the tips opposite. Allow to dry before attaching your sugar flower decorations.

Tips for hand piping polka dots and positioning flowers

o Measure the circumference of each tier, and work out how to divide it up equally. Mark out the position for your regularly spaced horizontal dots by gently pressing into the icing with a cocktail stick.

o Next, mark out how many vertical dots you can fit on each tier in the same way. I usually start piping designs such as this at the back of the cake, in case I make any mistakes and need to fix them or start again. Test out your piping this way, then proceed slowly to the front of the cake.

o If you're planning a more elaborate pattern, that might need more precision, such as the placement of the garland of sugar flowers on this cake, measure it out on a strip of paper, and pin the paper to the cake, before marking out.

o Use both hands when piping. Your dominant hand should hold the main part of the bag, and the index finger of your other hand can gently guide the tip of the metal nozzle.

o Keep a damp cloth and a clean, sharp-pointed knife nearby. If you make a mistake, gently scrape off the rubbish bit of icing with the knife and start again!

Creating the rolled sugar roses, sugar flowers and leaves

Using the same technique as on pages 64–66, colour, roll out and cut out a selection of sugar flowers and leaves in your favourite colours.

For the rolled sugar roses, roll out a long, thin strip of flower paste as thin as you can get it, then trim strips that are around 1 cm/⅓ inch thick. A wavy, irregular line works better for a more naturalistic effect. Carefully, using clean hands, roll the strip into a tight spiral, gently teasing out the outside edges to resemble petals. I often cut the bottom of each flower off with a sharp pair of scissors, so that I have a flat base to attach to the cake.

Attach the flowers to the cake with a little dot of royal icing, to secure.

LEFTOVERS AND LITTLE EXTRAS

LEFTOVER CAKE ICE LOLLIES

MAKES 6–10 ICE LOLLIES, DEPENDING ON THE SIZE OF THE MOULDS USED

Ingredients

6 scoops of low-fat vanilla frozen yoghurt (regular ice cream works well too)

4–6 tbsp milk
(or non-dairy milk)

1 tsp vanilla-bean extract (mint extract also works well)

1–2 tbsp sprinkles or chocolate vermicelli of your choosing (see page 44 for the home-made sprinkle recipe)

6–12 tbsp leftover cake crumbs (frozen, if you have them)

Ice-lolly moulds

Wooden ice-lolly sticks

To decorate

200 g/7 oz/1⅓ cups dark/milk chocolate, melted

Extra sprinkles

We make a lot of party and wedding cakes at Bee's Bakery, and to ensure that the partygoers get only the best, tastiest cake at their party, we trim off the edges, tops and bottoms of our cakes. This normally leaves us with a giant, dangerous bowl of leftover crumbs, chunks and knobbly bits, and I hate throwing them away, so I've been looking for some fun ways to use them up . . . and here are two!

You can easily freeze cake crumbs or chunks in a sandwich bag for use later – they last at least one month. Or, if you don't have any cake leftovers, but would like to try these recipes anyway, any old cake will do . . . and they're still delicious.

Dollop the frozen yoghurt or ice cream, milk, vanilla and sprinkles into a large bowl and mix until smooth. You're looking for a consistency of well-melted ice cream, here.

Add in your cake crumbs and mix as little as possible to avoid breaking up the bigger pieces – I prefer to have a variety of smaller and larger pieces so you can really get the texture when you bite into your lolly.

Pour the mixture into the lolly moulds and insert the sticks to around two-thirds of the way in.

Carefully put your lollies into the freezer and allow to freeze for around 3–5 hours before serving.

If you really want to jazz them up before serving, melt some milk or dark chocolate and pour on to the top of the ice lolly, letting it drizzle down the edges. Add a few sprinkles on top and serve!

LEFTOVER CAKE TRUFFLES

MAKES AT LEAST 10 TRUFFLES

<u>You will need</u>

Cake scraps, trimmings and offcuts to the
   equivalent of approximately 1 x 20-cm/
   8-inch round cake layer
4 tbsp vanilla (or other) buttercream (see recipe
   on page 32)
300 g/10½ oz/2 cups white, milk or dark chocolate,
   melted (this quantity will cover the volume of
   cake above)
Paste food colouring (optional)
Sprinkles or chopped nuts (optional)

Line a baking tray with parchment and ensure you have a shelf free
in your fridge/freezer for chilling the truffles.

Using your hands, break, crumble and tear your pieces of cake in
a large bowl until you have fine cake crumbs – if you have a few
different types of cake, use different bowls to keep the colours and
recipes separate.

Mix in the buttercream icing until well combined – the mixture
should now be a little sticky and come together in balls.

Using your hands, form small round balls about the size of a
walnut. Pop these on to your baking tray and, when you've used up
all the mixture, pop the baking tray in the fridge/freezer to hang out
for at least an hour whilst you make the coating.

In a bain-marie (a glass bowl perched on top of a pan of gently
simmering water), or a microwave, gently melt your chocolate,
adding colouring if you like.

Dip your cake balls into the chocolate and gently move around
with a teaspoon to coat. Fish them out and place back on the
parchment-lined tray to set.

Decorate with sprinkles/nuts before they set hard, and consume
within one week.

HOW TO MAKE YOUR OWN CAKE STANDS

You will need

A selection of different-sized plates (one per cake stand) – plastic and glass both work well, as long as they're not too heavy

Cool old dessert or cocktail glasses (one per cake stand), e.g. ones that you'd get ice cream in, in an old-fashioned restaurant (NB: for smaller cakes, thin-stemmed glasses work fine, but for larger/ heavier cakes, it's better to have short and fat glasses with shortish stems, as they're less likely to tumble over)

Silicon household sealant

Coloured spray paint (and possibly frosted spray paint to use to "prime" your glass plates/stands for the coloured paint)

Doilies/napkins/parchment
(to place in between the cake and the stand when you display your cakes, as the spray won't be food safe)

A protected work surface
(e.g. lined with newspaper)

Not everyone has a spare wodge of money to throw at the beautiful pale-green cake stand that's in all the magazines, and so what if you don't! Why not get creative and just make one of your own? In principle, it's super easy, doesn't require too much expensive kit, and, once you've mastered it, think of all the supercool birthday presents you can make for your friends!

Make sure the plates/glasses are clean before you start, and then coat the rim of the glass with a thick line of silicon sealant. Flip your plate upside down and press the glass firmly down on to it, in the middle of the underside, and allow to dry according to the silicon instructions (this bit might need to be left overnight). You might want to scrape away any sealant that squidges out, for neatness, but I think it's best to leave it, to make sure the seal is as strong as possible.

Once the sealant is properly dry, spray paint the stand in your chosen colour and allow to dry again, according to the instructions on the spray-paint can.

Before use, make sure you use a doily/piece of parchment to protect the cake from the paint.

Gently wipe the stands clean/hand wash in warm water, if needed, after use.

EDIBLE ICING PAPER CAKE TOPPER CHARACTERS

You will need

Edible fondant icing paper (available online)

Edible-ink marker pens

Sharp knife (a clean craft knife, if you have one)

Cutting board

Pastry brush

Piping gel

Sugar-paste icing or flower paste (this is a hard-setting version of sugar paste, but it's quite expensive and not essential)

Baking tray lined with parchment

A small amount of stiff-peak royal icing (see page 34)

We bake lots of bespoke designs for kids' cakes at Bee's Bakery, but, to be honest, I might have had my fill of requests for Disney-themed cakes! I long for more traditional illustrated characters, and these designs for cake toppers are influenced by this.

I am officially a terrible illustrator, and I need all sorts of help drawing even basic things, so I find printable outlines of animals online and carefully trace them on to edible paper using edible ink pens. You can trace your child's favourite character from a book or movie, or write their name or age for a more personal touch.

Edible icing paper is really easy to use, as are edible ink markers (both available online). It is best to let the illustrated icing set hard overnight, so begin the project at least one day before you need it, if you can.

First, print your designs on to standard printer paper, and then trace them on to edible paper using edible marker pens, going over any lines that needed to be stronger.

To make the images "stand up" as cake toppers, you'll need to roll out some white sugar paste, and coat the back of your edible paper with piping gel, then carefully stick it to the sugar paste, making sure there are no bubbles.

Cut carefully around the outline of your design. Place on the baking tray lined with parchment and leave to dry overnight, or for up to 3 days.

When ready to serve, gently lift the dried shapes from the tray and secure them to your cake with a little stiff-peak royal icing.

DIY GLITTER NAME TOPPERS

For the toppers, you will need

Plain neutral-coloured craft card
 and coarse craft glitter
 or pre-glittered card
Cutting mat
Craft knife
White craft glue
Pencil
Your chosen word or shape,
 printed in different font styles
 (of course, you can freestyle
 this by handwriting the word!)
Sharp scissors
Ruler
BBQ skewers/long cocktail sticks

These are inspired by my buddy, Charlie Philips, who I worked with on styling all the supercool pictures in this book and my first book, *Bee's Brilliant Biscuits*. Charlie is an amazing prop stylist and is great at making awesome paper things – from cards and paper chains, to backgrounds and sets – and she made the lovely little card toppers in the Mothers' Day Splatter Cake recipe (see page 62).

There are no real limits to what you can "DIY" in terms of cake toppers, and there are a million free fonts, printables and designs available online that you can use as stencils, so get creative!

To create your glitter shapes

Print or sketch the words and shapes that you'd like on to your craft card, and, using a craft knife or a sharp pair of scissors, carefully cut around the words or shapes. You can also freestyle the writing by hand, but I print and trace the letters to get a really smart-looking shape!

Stick your words or shapes on to the skewers with craft glue and allow to dry for at least 1 hour. Consider using 2 skewers to give extra support to longer words/ larger shapes.

If you're using plain card that needs to be "glittered up", paint a thin layer of white glue on to one side of the topper, and sprinkle a generous layer of glitter over the top – I tend to do this on top of a paper plate/piece of paper so I can easily transfer leftover glitter back into the pot for using again. Repeat on the other side of your shape word, then tap a few times to shake off any excess glitter before allowing to dry for at least 1 hour.

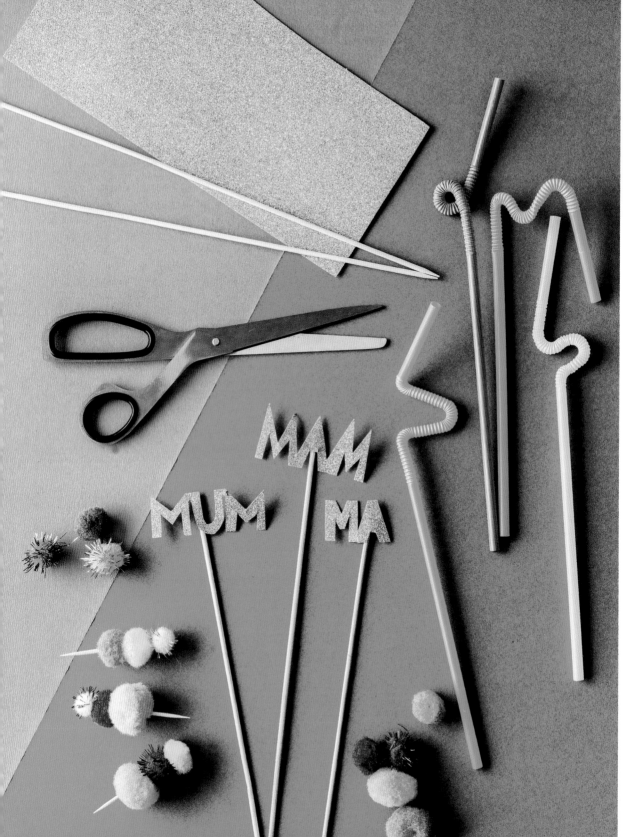

INDEX

THANK YOUS

I run the business part of this baking gig by myself, which often means my mates are bombarded by random texts asking absurd questions along the lines of, "Will you drive to an industrial estate in the rain with me?" "Can you test this unsweetened cauliflower-cake recipe?" "Can I borrow your dog for the photo shoot?" So, first of all, I need to say a mega, extra, super-massive thank you, high five, and give an awkwardly long hug to everyone who's encouraged and supported me since I started four years ago . . . throughout the process of my first book, *Bee's Brilliant Biscuits*, to this one.

Some days (tax-return days not included), I honestly think I have the best job in the world – baking cakes for parties and weddings, testing and writing recipes, and making beautiful pictures with my dream team. It's a fantastic job and I'm very grateful indeed to tons of people, including the following:

Charlie Philips, you are a prop-styling guru and I love working with you, every single shoot we do; and Liz and Max Haarala-Hamilton, somehow you manage to take brilliant pictures of our wack creations that look so striking and really capture the mood.

Emily Preece-Morrison and all at Pavilion Books, I can't thank you enough for taking yet another punt on this mad little scientist-turned-baker. I love what I do and wouldn't be able to do it without you – so a million thank yous, and slices of mad cake for pudding too.

Thank you to Dominique for superb assistance in the bakery and on our shoots – you are a baking demon, and a joy to have around.

Thank you to Milly Withington, Rachel Conway, Georgina Capel and Simon Shaps at Capel & Associates for "taking me on"!

Big kitchen love to my gang of food-business buddies: James Hughes-Davies (www.ljhorners.com), Michael Gratz (www.prairiefirebbq.com), Jez Felwick (www.thebowler.co.uk), Andreia and Luis-Carlos, Dixie and Will (www.aphroditesfood.com). Thanks to Allie and Ellen at Hedley & Bennett (www.hedleyandbennett.com) for my smashing aprons.

Thank you to Mr Bee's Bakery – Dan – for gracefully overlooking the constant dusting of flour our kitchen gets, the regular coercion to try new cakes with "surprise" (vegetable) ingredients, and for your legendary end-of-shoot mobile cocktail-bar service. You're the best!

And finally, merci beaucoup to my mum, Sandra, who persists at testing recipes for me, despite an extremely strong aversion to baking and following instructions.

STOCKISTS

First published in the United Kingdom in 2017
by Pavilion
43 Great Ormond Street
London
WC1N 3HZ

Text © Bee Berrie, 2017
Design and layout © Pavilion Books
Company Ltd, 2017
Photography © Pavilion Books Company
Ltd, 2017

The moral rights of the author have been
asserted.

ISBN: 978-1-91121-624-7

A CIP catalogue record for this book is
available from the British Library.

10 9 8 7 6 5 4 3 2 1

Reproduction by Mission, Hong Kong
Printed and bound by Toppan Leefung
Printing Ltd, China

This book can be ordered direct from the
publisher at www.pavilionbooks.com

Baking kit

Nisbets – for professional quality (and priced) kit
(www.nisbets.co.uk)

Cake Craft Shop for tins, paste colours, all sorts of jazzy
equipment (www.cakecraftshop.co.uk)

A Piece of Cake Thame – an old fashioned shop, great for
stocking up on sugar flower kit (www.sugaricing.com)

Paperchase – for all sorts of lovely craft papers and paper-
flower-making gadgets (www.paperchase.co.uk)

Ingredients

Asda are great for general ingredients and very keenly priced
(www.groceries.asda.com)

Ocado has by far the widest range of top quality ingredients for
those with a few more pennies (www.ocado.com)

Healthy supplies – brilliant source of healthier baking
ingredients, including fruit and superfood powders
(www.healthysupplies.co.uk)

Holland and Barret have a good stock of (quite expensive) vegan
ingredients (www.hollandandbarrett.com)

Beautiful baking clothes

Aprons – the most badass aprons I've ever seen come from
Hedley & Bennett (www.hedleyandbennett.com)

Edible flowers

For certified organic flowers, grown by a Soil Association hero
on the most beautiful farm I've ever seen – ask Jan at Maddocks
Farm (www.maddocksfarmorganics.co.uk)